Creating Something from Nothing

How to Never Lose Via the Reverse

By Kenneth F. George

Order this book online at www.trafford.com
or email orders@trafford.com

Most Trafford titles are also available at major online book retailers.

Printed in the United States of America.

ISBN: 978-1-4269-7408-3 (sc)
ISBN: 978-1-4269-7409-0 (e)

Library of Congress Control Number: 2011910773

Trafford rev. 07/06/2011

 www.trafford.com

North America & international
toll-free: 1 888 232 4444 (USA & Canada)
phone: 250 383 6864 ♦ fax: 812 355 4082

Reviews

"Masterpiece!" – Ken George

"Amazing piece of literature…a work of art!" – Ken George

"A legend in my own mind." – Ken George

"Encore! Bravo!" – Ken George

"Exceptional writing…the second best book ever written..." – Ken George

"The greatest book I never read!" – to quote Lord Shakespeare, my cat

Dedicated to my mother
Amelia George

Special thanks to my ghost writer
Patricia GW

Contents

Introduction

It was the best of times, it was the worst——whoops, wrong book!

Let's get this straight right now: I'll be the first to say this book won't go down in history as a literary classic. You only paid roughly the price of a fast food burger and shake to buy it, so you're already ahead – I've saved you from gaining a pound or two. So please hold any lightweight prejudgment until after you've read it.

Now that I've already criticized you the reader, before you had a chance to criticize this book, you've just had your first lesson in the sales closing technique I used on prospects called THE REVERSE.

The Reverse is one of the greatest concepts I ever came up with. It is generally the opposite of what a prospect is expecting. It was never indigenous just to closing techniques; it became a way of life in and around the sale, outside the sale, and in the events that happened. They were all Reverses.

When I finally realized it was part of my sales philosophy, it became even easier.

The concepts of the Reverse I introduce in this book are interlocking. Since they directly or indirectly affected everything I did in sales, you will see the same techniques brought up again in multiple chapters. Just as I repeated myself to the prospect to make sure they understood, I've repeated myself throughout this book for you the Reader to understand. Stay awake and you'll get it.

Read on – who knows? You may even learn something as well as enjoy it. Either way, no refund.

Disclaimer

I've chosen not to name any persons, places, or specific monetary figures to protect the innocent (or the guilty). This information has been generalized, so save time and leave your lawyer alone with any idea of a lawsuit. He's probably too busy chasing ambulances anyway.

Although this is an instructional book for sales types who want to learn more about the Reverse, I'm sure the average reader may find the concepts of the Reverse insightful also.

Adrenaline Rush

Here I am on stage receiving honored awards for being the National Sales Housing Champion of the Year. I'm wearing a tuxedo with cameras going off at a high end hotel in some exotic location, thinking *how did this all begin?* Possibly my mind was going back to when I was the top paperboy in my district and winning trips all over the country. I hadn't known then that selling was my true calling.

Upon graduating as a high school senior class president, I started out in industry with a flunky clerk's job. I attended night school to get my degree at the same time. I never worked so hard in all my life as I did as a clerk. I had no raise for years and then was laid off. The corporation called me back to another job as a flunky clerk, only this time I had the glorified title of "engineer" and that's only because a good man had to die first for me to get the promotion.

I was laid off again in the following years, but now I had a family to support. When I was called back again, I was put into a training program for the same corporation. Because I could speak fairly well, I was made a general foreman overnight with several foremen under me, each of them smarter than I was about the factory.

I avoided the next layoff by making a lateral move as an instructor to the Hard Core Training Program that was developed in response to the race riots that had flared up in the city. I saw there was a clandestine meeting of middle management going on. Someway somehow I got an invite to sit in on the meeting as a guest, and was told by my supervisor to keep my mouth shut because I sounded like a used car salesman.

The so-called executives had a paradigm on the wall of a proposed program whose main purpose was to train the guys that burnt down the city to work in the factory on the assembly line. To tell you the truth, the people in these meetings who came off as well-intentioned were just as much opportunists. I would classify myself as a bit of both also.

Seeing it all mapped out on the wall, with a charged up attitude I asked why they hadn't done it yet. It was the obvious question. The response was they were waiting for a PhD to come in and implement the program. It was well known that the minority middle management guys who controlled the committee only wanted a minority guy to control the training program.

With my adrenaline flowing, I convinced them to let me take on the task of implementing it instead. Apparently I had them under ether so well that one of them yelled out, "Who cares about the program? We're for Ken George!" Quite a Reverse, eh?

Management immediately gave me the program after I said I would write it in one week. Actually it took me only four days, and I'm not a writer – another Reverse. This told me it wasn't how good I was, it was how bad they were. They were afraid to make a mistake and didn't want to rock the boat.

Once the program was implemented, I received commendations from two vice presidents from the company. When the local news station came in with their cameras to see how we were doing with the program, the trainees who burnt down the city hid their faces because they were wanted for several charges for various crimes around the country. The factory brought in a lot of high tech equipment to train them. The trainees would come back at night to steal it and sell it back to us the next morning for a dime on the dollar.

Now the deal was this: as long as the corporation could keep these guys on the job for one year, the word was the government would reimburse the corporation. This way, they wouldn't be down in the city lighting matches. When these guys were put on the assembly line, it gave every foreman in the plant a near heart attack. They screwed up the vehicles so bad they took one of the car lines from one plant and put it over the border where it could be manufactured safely.

Eventually there was another layoff and I left the corporation for good.

"Go Out and Get Bloodied"

With a family to support, I immediately checked the want ads in the newspaper. One ad read: "Sales Reps Wanted!" All I had to do was put on a presentation of the service offered; I didn't have to sell anything for the company to pay me. I made several presentations, but the

Reverse was the prospects were actually buying the service! After a month I was the top producer in the office. I asked one of the other top producers how he did that month, and he came back at me with, "What are you, a smartass?" I was naive – I thought everyone could do what I could do.

Eventually I was approached by a manager who was trying to recruit me into recreational land sales. He spent about 45 minutes trying to con me into the deal. I finally told him, "You could have saved your energy, I came here to be hired." A Reverse!

Not wanting to waste much time in the training, he took me out the same night to watch a presentation. His condition was that I had to keep my mouth shut. I watched him as he made the sale. When it was over and we were out the door, he said to me, "Okay kid, you've been trained. Go out and get bloodied." He handed me a lead.

I went out that night, made a presentation, and wrote the deal.

It awed the whole office. Of course, with a contest on that month I ended up winning again as the top producer. It really excited me... until I found out my manager and another top producer named "Sweet Willy" came up with a scheme to extend the contest so I would come in second, behind him.

Let me paint a picture of this character: Sweet Willy wore a toupee, had store-bought teeth and sported an instant suntan he got using an aluminum shield, gazing at the sun while sitting in his car in the parking lot. He wore lifts in his shoes and pads on his shoulders. He was not exactly a paragon of virtue.

Sweet Willy wasn't just the top producer in the office, he was number one in the whole company and had been for several years. He was an icon in the business; they even named a street after him.

Now Willy was a great guy. He wanted to help everybody, especially the new guys. The first thing he would do is ask them, "Can I help you? Now I don't mean to be abrasive..." and then proceeded to be abrasive. It gave him the license to impose his opinions. When Willy wanted to help somebody, it was like Hitler asking for peace. A piece of Poland, a piece of France, you get the message. This was the start of the head games.

Willy had such an intimidating reputation in the office some of the guys at the office wanted to set up a phony lead so they could hide in the back room just to hear how he pitched his deals. They were all awed by Willy, and so was I until he stole that contest from me.

When I realized I'd won the contest that first month, Sweet Willy put his arm around me saying, "You know kid, I could easily write my son the doctor on a huge contract and would have won this contest."

"Yes," I said, "but that wouldn't have been competitive."

"Yes, you're right," he said. "I just couldn't bring myself to do a thing like that."

Afterwards, I was driving home when it occurred to me that I'd left something back at the office. When I returned, the receptionist ran up to me and said, "Do you know what Willy did? He wrote his son the doctor on a contract! The manager extended the contest so you came in second."

When I heard how they screwed me, it was like a hot poker stuck in my gut. Sweet Willy then walked up and put his arm around me saying, "Kid, you're in shark-infested waters. Go back to a 9-to-5 job where it's safe."

Willy had said he wouldn't write his son the doctor, and he'd already pulled the scam off as he was telling me! Here's the real zinger: after Willy got his bonus from "winning" the contest, his son the doctor canceled the contract.

With his arm still on my shoulders, Willy said to me in his smug tone, "We shouldn't be enemies, we should be friends."

It was a game changing moment. He didn't know that when he said that to me, I had an epiphany. If I beat him once, I could beat him again. I no longer looked at Willy as a god in the business nor was willing to settle for second banana when I knew what I was capable of. I made a personal commitment, motivated within myself right then and there, to take this guy down.

Instead of blowing me out of sales, the Reverse was I realized my potential and became one of the best in the business.

Reader, stay awake for the next exciting chapter!

Showdown at the OK Corral

I learned another good lesson from that first contest: never tell anybody what I'm doing. I couldn't trust anyone anymore in that office. I knew that if I were to stay in the business of sales, I had to play my cards close to the vest and keep a low profile. I couldn't tell anyone – not even my manager – what my progress was on how many deals I was making, until the right moment. I was no longer naïve. I became an island unto myself.

Now that I got it, I knew I was among conmen in a den of thieves who played head games.

The next month was the biggest contest in the local office, and the Vice President of the company was coming to give the award to the top producer. Oh, and did I mention that the VP was also Sweet Willy's cousin? If Willy was possibly not at the top of his game in the first contest that I technically won, you could bet he was going to be going full speed in this next contest, especially with his cousin coming to town. If it was a fluke that he was not as dangerous in the last contest, he would be the prince of darkness in this one.

Willy's ego was at stake. He had to be wondering how a nobody upstaged him to begin with. He was going to make sure this stroke of luck didn't have an encore performance. In fact, I'm sure he couldn't wait to beat me badly to put me in my place, just for the revenge alone.

I wanted Willy and my manager to think I was just a flash in the pan the previous contest. They had no idea what I was up to because I didn't give them any indication about my performance. By acting like a Greek tragedy they thought I was just another green salesman on his way to being broomed out like a beaten dog.

While this was going on at the office, I was secretly writing contracts as if I was possessed. For the entire month, every time I made a sale I would say to myself, "You're going down, Willy." I was driven, yet acted numb and dumb at the office.

My manager would say to me, "What happened? You were off to a good start in the last contest. Any business this month?" I'd shake my head. The other salesman saw this, and muttered around that I was just lucky the first month.

In reality, I kept stacking up those contracts. In order to cover myself, I told the prospects I wrote that it would take 30 days to process their deals. This way I wouldn't blow my cover. If those deals had come into the office immediately, everyone would have known what I was doing.

In Willy's mind he was very confident that he'd already won. He'd been taking the top spot in the contests by default for the past decade. This was partly due to the fact Willy and my manager were teaming up as partners in crime. My manager would write deals in Willy's name, and made overrides on the other salespeople as well as me. They would discuss over eggs how Willy was going to take the next contest.

The whole office was intimidated by Willy's ego. He would mess with their heads by aligning all of his plaques and awards on the wall. He was very humble that way. He'd flash around the contracts he wrote in front of the struggling salespeople, acting as if he didn't know that he was overwhelming them. He'd broom out 5 or 6 salespeople that way then say, "I'm sorry to lose that guy, he was a fine gentlemen," as if he really cared. A salesperson who quit was one less competitor for Willy.

After aligning his plaques for the day, Willy would ask the secretary if there had been any calls for him. If it was a grief call – a prospect looking for Willy because they didn't like the deal he sold them – he'd whisper, "I'm not in." He'd then go back to the manager to pick up fresh leads he could cream for easy deals. It was something rarely anyone else got their hands on, especially me.

Willy played his role, and I played mine. Everyone had a part. I felt like I was a producer on Broadway, pulling the strings on these puppets, with Willy acting the lead role and my manager as supporting actor. In reality I was playing my own part, and I was going to win the Academy Award.

In those 30 days my adrenaline was flowing and I felt like I'd take off into the sky. On the outside, I kept up a moping, negative attitude for effect. I could hardly wait for the day of the reckoning to even the score. Let me reiterate that I never thought or even believed back then that the national hero of the company could be taken down by anyone, last of all myself.

I would do the same thing back in my days as a newspaper boy. I would sandbag my competitors by not turning in all my starts to my paper route manager. Starts were new customers signed on to receive the newspaper. I played the coy routine until the very last moment, and then overwhelmed the other carriers with the business I turned in. This is how I won many of the contests when I was a paperboy.

So you see, this pirate Willy was not just playing his head games, he was playing mine. The difference was I honed my skills at a very young age.

I suspect that after going blank for three weeks with no deals, the manager was telling Willy to just write me off. You have to understand, in creative sales it's just a numbers game. They throw bodies against the wall to see what sticks. From my manager's standpoint, he already got the last ounce of juice out of me in the last contest.

Judgment Day

It was finally the day of the contest. I had written such a volume of business that my briefcase was loaded with contracts. I had never delivered a single one to the office, holding them to the last moment. What I was doing was sandbagging Willy and everybody else.

Being the fox he was, on the last day of the contest Willy brought in a batch of contracts also. He turned them face-down on the desk so nobody could see what they were worth. I worried he had done it to me again. However, being the conniver *I was*, I had Willy paged out of his office so I could sneak in and tip over the contracts. They were blanks.

"Wow. I got you, Willy," I said to myself. I knew I had him beat.

At that moment, everyone was called into the meeting for the contest of the year. I started to walk into the meeting room when my manager came over to me.

"This is it," he said. "Do you have any deals at all? You better turn them in now."

I called him into a private room and said, "Is this enough?" as I *slowly* poured out those contracts in front of him. I saw the look on his face – he was shocked.

After my manager turned in the count, I went into the meeting room. I sat down in the last chair in the last row. The other salespeople had already filed in and were waiting for the VP to honor the winner of the contest.

Sweet Willy was sitting in the front row adjusting his tie, grinning. He was dressed to the nines. I happened to be dressed very low profile, with a T-shirt and sandals. The VP looked me over and muttered to my manager, "We can't have guys looking like that around here."

The VP acknowledged us, saying there had been a record set for the highest number of individual sales. Everybody looked around, wondering who had pulled off this unique feat. They knew it wasn't Willy – he was known for writing big ticket contracts, not a lot of smaller ones.

They're turning around to one another, wondering who won. While they were turning around, I was too. I savored the moment, not giving any indication it was me.

Finally, the VP announced my name. I walked up front very slowly from the back, looking the VP right in the eye. I saw the shock on his face as he realized I was the guy he didn't want there because of the way I was dressed. I took the award and walked it by Willy's face, waving the check under his nose. He turned white and I thought his toupee flipped.

I had scammed the scammers!

Looking back, Willy screwing me out of the first contest was the most significant thing to happen to me in sales. It was the best thing he could have ever done for me. Being bushwhacked out of the first contest lit me up like a rocket. I never felt that charged up in my life. During the rest of our career while we were in the same office, Sweet Willy and I ran in the top-two in terms of production.

All I'd wanted to do was make a living in sales. I hadn't realized what I was capable of until I made the personal commitment to be the best I could be and dethrone Willy. I had just felt honored to be in the same office with him. As I said, I was naïve, but more important is the fact I was motivated more by a loss than by a victory. That's a great Reverse! I suspect to find out how good someone can be they must first have a baptism of fire through some adversity. If you're just coasting comfortably in life, there is little motivation to improve. However when someone rocks your boat, your adrenaline is flowing and your survival skills kick in, as mine did.

Now that I'd found my station in life, there was another gunslinger in town. From thereon in, it was a perpetual showdown at the OK Corral between Willy and I.

Control: The Key to the Close

Reader, let me ask you what I often ask the salespeople in my seminars: *When do you think control begins?*

Almost invariably I would hear the response that control begins at the initial part of the pitch. Right?

Wrong. *A Reverse!*

Control starts before you even leave the post. With control, you can erase all the pressure from yourself and transfer it onto the prospect. Without it, there's only a 50-50 shot that you'll close the deal, and I don't like those odds.

To maintain control, you simply have to do something that's not expected. In other words, you have to *Reverse* them. The "Reverse" is part of the philosophy of selling. The prospect has heard pitches before and is prepared with the ammunition of every possible objection. If the prospect can predict your presentation, he's in control. And if he's control, you my friend are out of control.

Now that you understand when control begins, you are free to realize you can never lose what you never had. It's not something you will understand immediately; you must do it a few times to believe it.

Before you leave the post, I feel you have to be in control of yourself with your lifestyle. That had a lot to do with what I accomplished. I tried to lead a balanced life. When you're continuously in control, you don't have to compartmentalize it for when you go to make a sale. I didn't say, "It's time to see a customer, now I'm going to take control of me." I was generally in control of my life.

The average fast-track closer that I met more or less put on a performance with control; it wasn't something that he lived with. Some of these guys were at the bar living life in the fast lane. Their whole lifestyle was out of balance as far as I saw it.

If you're out of control, you probably have credit card people chasing your butt and you're late on your alimony payments, as many sales types are. If that's the case, you don't even know what control is. Many salespeople seem to be amoral, not even caring if they were right or wrong – they were way beyond that. They got to a point where there were no rules, and they weren't losing sleep over it either.

Some of them would spin a few tales to the prospect to seal a deal. When they pulled these scams, they were in effect stereotyping all other salespeople which made my job harder. Immediately I had to fight off an image from the prospect that I hadn't earned.

Control handles setbacks and cancellations. I counted on myself. I don't remember any manager offering any support. As I pointed out earlier, it was generally a do-or-die operation. When you're in creative sales, you usually don't have unions or management support. You're on your own. You more or less control your own destiny. When I was alone in the office, it was up to me to master plan my own strategies. Even if some of these sales managers *wanted* to help, they were generally too inept. They didn't have an inkling of how to really write a deal. They were never shy about taking my overrides however, or taking credit for my performance when they reported back to the home office.

I did not see much if any honor in most of the characters in these sales offices, so I presented an image that I wanted to be on my own. I generally stayed away from them as much as possible around the office, and certainly would not hang out with them when they were out carousing at night. I did not resent those who did not have any sales ability, but it seemed they resented me because of mine.

Many people initially join sales because they are on the rebound after they've lost their job and their so-called "guarantees." They find out quickly that life can deal some cruel cards when trying to pay their bills is contingent on their sales performance. Either way, they're still required to carry their own weight. They have to resolve their financial obligations to provide for their family with the three biological necessities of food, shelter, and clothing.

Creative sales seems to have no middle ground. You can either close or you can't. Unfortunately most of the closers I encountered had a problem with their sales ethics. They said or did anything to make a deal. As for myself, I was guilty of hubris. At times I was guilty of the sin of omission as well. It was what I *didn't* say. Not lying – I was too proud to lie. But with the slick-talking closers, it was the sin of omission *and* commission. They couldn't go back and face the prospect a second time. I never had that problem.

Control is a funny thing. Whenever you go through a sales drought, you begin to doubt your own ability. The question "will I ever write another deal?" would go through my mind, and any other salespersons who would admit it. It's the same for athletes who go into a slump and begin to doubt they will be able to perform at the level that they used to with their abilities. The best thing you can do is get right back into sales with another presentation as soon as possible. This is when you have to maintain your momentum. You don't want to shake your confidence, which is where character counts.

Control projects confidence. It doesn't give off signals to prospects that you live or die by any deal. If anybody is going to sweat it's going to be the guy across the table. If you have a lifestyle that allows for most setbacks, you can still survive when there are no potential deals coming your way. Even after losing a big deal – and yes, it will sting – as you get over it you're even stronger for the next sale, not weaker. That's a Reverse.

I'm well aware that hotshot closers generate the big production numbers in any sales office, but how is it that at the end of the day many of these producers seem to be on the bottom with their personal life and creditors chasing them? After they blow their money at the casinos, on booze, the ladies, and sports bets, they're pockets are empty but the wolves are still at the door.

There's a big difference between being in first place and being number one. That's a Reverse. I suspect creative sales organizations in the long run are better off with the second-

and third-place producers who have a solid performance, rather than a first-place closer with personal problems. When creditors are on their trail, closers get desperate. They give grievous misrepresentations during their pitch to make a sale, which can come back to haunt the sales office. This is all because they are out of control with their personal lives.

Sales training manuals are all about how to pitch, but they don't teach how to control your lifestyle. That's why more salespeople appear to fail than succeed. The more control you have, the more you project to the prospect.

If you live a fast-track lifestyle, it's a hit-or-miss proposition and you're intimidated by the prospect. He's sitting there on his throne waiting for the next dummy to come knocking on his door. He has all these objections ready, just waiting to play god in front of his wife. It didn't work with me because I only counted on one person and that was myself. I knew what I would say; I would simply Reverse the prospect by telling him he was the expert. So all the ammunition the prospect wanted to use on me was neutralized. That's one way how I gained control so quickly— I generally knew what the prospect was going to say to me.

Team Effort: You're On Your Own

If you think it may not be politically correct to ignore the team-spirit routine, consider this: I never saw a team rescue me on the many winter nights I was driving down a country road, chasing a lead. Some big semi would often get right on top of me and nearly run me into a ditch! When I arrived at the prospect's house, several times I was stood up. Even if I did pitch the prospect and wrote the deal, sometimes they cancelled it the next day. I didn't see any team helping me when I was going through all of that.

Creative sales is a place where you either stand up on your own or you go down. I understood the tenets, and I accepted them. The team approach is a lot of crap. I think some creative sales organizations dumb down the troops with the false hope of this team effort. After all, the companies had a revolving door policy with an ongoing recruiting process. They threw bodies against the wall to see what stuck. While they're doing this mass recruiting, most sales organizations don't tell the neophytes about the pitfalls of going into the profession. It's the sin of omission.

Even though I criticized them for doing it, I loved the drama. I couldn't wait to get up in the morning and go to the mine fields. That was part of the game. It gave me an adrenaline rush. I loved to create my own master plan and see it come to fruition. That's when you know you're in control.

As successful creative salespeople, we are probably one of the last of the rugged individualists. We have no one to support us – not any company, union, or other safety net. The most valuable thing that this country offers is opportunity, as most any immigrant who's moved here will tell you. For anyone here not to take advantage of opportunity if they have talent and ambition is their loss.

One of the requests that I always bargained for when I was hired in to a sales office was that I did not want to sit in on any time-consuming, pathetic sales meetings. I'm not aware of any sale ever being written in a sales meeting. Putting me in a sales meeting was like handcuffing me from writing deals because out in the trenches I could out-perform most of my competitors. Now Reader that may sound egotistical and independent, but I don't apologize for my audacity.

The managers went along with my request for no meetings, but all of them eventually went back on their word. This would cause a lot of resentment by the other salespeople because they thought I was acting like a prima donna. All I was guilty of was writing deals.

On one occasion the general manager sucked me into a rah-rah meeting for a sales contest to see who could set the most appointments first. They singled me out because I wasn't going through the gyrations like the rest of them. They saw my low profile as a sign of weakness. Eventually my manager said, "You think you're better than the rest of us? Get involved!"

The rest of the salespeople jeered me on to join the contest. I didn't want to be a part of it. I knew there were no closers among them – in other words, no Willy's. I told them, "You don't want me in this contest."

When they kept pushing the issue, I realized I wasn't getting any respect from this office.

"Fine," I said. "I'll join the contest, but on *my rules*: me against the whole office! You're outnumbered."

I figured I might as well shove it down their throats, seeing as they were all having such a great time at my expense. They thought I was a real smart@$$ saying I would take on the whole office, but I was serious. They accepted the bet, with the prize being dinner at a very nice restaurant.

"I will win this contest and enjoy that meal," I said, and walked out of the meeting into my office. What these other salespeople obviously didn't know was that I could set leads at will with the Yellow Pages.

On the phone I told potential prospects, "Hello Mrs. Jones, there's been a glitch in the computer and your name came up spelled wrong. There will be a clerk dropping by your house this evening to correct the error, and we haven't been able to reach him. Could you please have him use your phone to call us back at the home office? Sorry for wasting your time." And that was my lead.

Within an hour of banging on the phone I had several appointments. Of course when that clerk showed up at their door, it would be *me* inside the prospect's house. I'd use their phone to call the home office, pitching the prospect as I talked on the phone about whatever it was I was selling.

Of course, I won the contest to the embarrassment of the lightweights. Although winning did not endear me to the office, I gained their respect.

The company had another team approach with a setup where they would allow two sales teams with a generous budget to pitch prospects with a free dinner, trying to sell them property. That's four salespeople to each team, wining and dining the prospect with their dog and pony show. The truth was there were a lot of moochers who were just there for the free dinner.

I had no budget, no free *anything*, and many times I outperformed entire sales teams. Time and again I wrote more deals than them without even leaving my office; I simply pitched over the phone.

When these sales teams struck out at their dinner parties, the office would dump their recycled leads on me.

When I received them and wrote a deal out of them – would you believe this! – those same parasites who couldn't write the deal to begin with would come back at me with the manager's approval, saying I had to split my commissions with them. These weasels were going to throw those leads in the garbage can anyway!

There was one occasion where I was at a prominent hotel where promoters were buying table time to present their products to the crowd. The prospects largely consisted of doctors who were hosting their national convention. My competitors had a huge display with overhead lights, and were wining and dining the doctors in their own hotel suites. They had brought their dinner party mentality to the national convention. As for myself, I just had a table and a map.

The convention was a three day event. After the second day, my competitors came over to me and flaunted their deals in my face. I had nothing. On the third day, close to quitting time, I walked away for about 20 minutes. When I came back, there was a postcard lying on my table. It said on the back: "I will give you a 5 minute presentation. Don't try to pressure me for this property, because I've heard about you from my doctor friends."

I called the phone number on the card and agreed to an appointment with the prospect. Upon going to his office, he looked me over and shook my hand.

"You have five minutes," he said.

After 5 minutes, we went to 15 minutes. After 15 minutes, we went to 45 minutes. At that point, he rocked back in his chair and laughed, saying, "Who's the analyst here, me or you?"

I took a huge deposit on a piece of commercial property. I did quite well that day, but again it's *not the end of the story*. That doctor, who wanted to give me 5 minutes with no pressure, not only bought a very expensive piece of property, he also gave me at least 10 referrals where I sold a combination of lots and condominiums. I wrote a great amount of business from that little card that was sitting on my desk. Not only that, but after the convention my competitors who had flaunted their contracts had their deals cancelled! I had created something from nothing again!

When you're in control you can take on a professional, and when you have sold them you're the professional.

Stress: Enemy #1

As I said, in any profession it's smart to be prepared with a balanced lifestyle. If you're hoping to close a sale to keep the wolves from the door, you're a fool. The stress of just hoping you can write the deal will drive you crazy. If you can't close, it's even worse. It's enough to send you back to the water hole to drink away your misery. Your life cannot operate on an if-come-maybe. A prospect can smell the fear on you, and generally no one wants to deal with a loser.

Stress can in fact work for or against you. In creative sales, if you're a closer then stress can feel similar to an adrenaline rush. For many green salespeople, it could be the road to a cardiac condition. To be fair and level the playing field, being a very democratic type of guy I would make sure that the prospect received his share of stress. It was an equal opportunity for everybody; I wouldn't want them to miss out.

During a pitch, I could see the flush in the prospect's face as beads of sweat came rolling down their foreheads. I was playing my head games with them. The logic they were counting on went out the window when I Reversed them to emotion.

The Reverse is the fast-track closer usually can't wait to go out and blow their commission. If that's the case, they'd go out and live large only to come home to empty wallets at the end of the day. That would give them a lot of stress. When it was time to pay the piper, they deserved what they got.

Where is this stress coming from? Aside from the managers, there was the competition from the slick closers who seemed to cream the leads from the top, and also competing sales organizations. Add on top of this the prospects whose ultimate weapon is the killer word *no*, and you have the finishing touches of the stress that discourages sales types.

The person who can do the worst damage, more than all the others combined, is – are you ready for this sales types? It's *you*. That's right. When you allow all this negative input to overwhelm you, you become your own worst enemy.

Whoever gave you the idea that creative sales was a walk in the park? Probably many of you were cast offs from the 9-to-5 layoffs where you were paid whether you performed or not. Maybe you were the type that looked down on salespeople, but now because your cushy job is gone you've decided to try sales yourself. Now that's a Reverse, isn't it?

Recently because of the economic tsunami, even up to 70% of all salespeople have retired their ticket. They've given up their real estate license and left the game. They survived in good times, but the real acid test is to survive in bad times. Just because you're having a bad day doesn't mean that anybody cares. They don't. Once a salesperson can accept this, they will really see that they are in a profession where you are all by yourself. Forget that team approach crap — I think it's just a crutch for the sales clerks. *You are a team of one.*

Creative sales is a war game where there are winners and losers. If you've been busy paying attention Reader, then you know I said I could not afford the luxury of losing, not with a family to support. I was not in sales for the love and affection of the prospects. Whether I closed or not, I made sure I came out the winner with style. That's control.

The average sales type doesn't have any concept of control if they are taught that being a good loser is in good taste. This isn't a game of tennis where you congratulate the opposition. If there was stress, it was on the prospect across the table.

I know 9-to-5 jobs do not teach how to handle stress, but creative sales will. If one does not have the control to cope with it, they will join the long list of whiners who will fall by the wayside. Nobody is going to do anything for you. Sure, they'll spin you a story about teamwork, but do they ever write a deal in your name? *No!* They might do it for their buddies if they're kicking back to them.

I feel that if you help me, you have weakened me. If anybody wanted to get involved with me to help, I rejected it. This is the same attitude I feel should be adopted by some laid off workers who are depending on the government for help all the time. Sure, it's nice when someone is there to help you, but what happens when that crutch is taken away?

You fall on your face! Why not help yourself? You must pay the price to pay the bills.

The most important concept of the Reverse is *control*. Utilizing the concept of the Reverse gives you control. It takes on a life of its own, not just in the sales arena but in your lifestyle. With control, I had the audacity to walk into any company without training and many times be able to negotiate a sale. You don't have the pressure or stress when you tell yourself you can't lose what you never had.

If any of your Readers do not understand what I mean when I say I never lose, call me for a seminar. I will go into great detail to explain it – 586-873-2987 *get smart, get me.*

Swimming with the Sharks

Most salespeople have one enemy to fight: the prospect in the field. I was up against two fronts. Not only was I combating the prospects, but I was up against the office and other salespeople who were using head games.

In the office there are two types of power: formal and informal. Formal power is given to the lightweight, parasitic managers that I met who would leech off the residuals of the salespeople that could write the deals. The managers were intimidated by the power the closers had to be able to write deals. Knowing they couldn't match up to the closers who were out in the trenches, they jealously guarded their titles because it was all they had.

As a closer, I had informal power even though I didn't want it. It was forced on me. I became the go-to guy because of my track record. It came down to this: smart people who knew they couldn't close their own leads would come to me and ask me to close their deals for a 50-50 split. Instead of stealing from me, the Reverse was now I got a piece of them for a change. I didn't mind splitting it with them — it was half of something I would have never had. That was the best position to be in.

It was a gratifying feeling to help some of the other salespeople who were struggling. I'm not saying I was being a good Samaritan, but it cost me nothing. It was a win-win for both of us. Certainly it inflated my ego that I knew something that they didn't. I didn't need their help, but at times they needed me. I wasn't there to be anyone's friend, but if they approached me for help I would gladly give it.

The Reverse was that usually the office was full of sales types who sucked up to one another and pretended to be real buddy-buddy. That is, until there was a deal involved. Then they'd act like a bunch of piranhas trying to eat each other. Personally I never felt that way because I didn't feel threatened by any of them. Certainly I could get more than annoyed whenever they tried to pirate one of my deals, but I was always motivated no matter what way they found to scam from me. All I had to do was write another deal. Outside of meeting my financial obligations, money was not my prime motive. Instead, it was to compete and win. Of course, the money came with it and I never turned it down.

Now there were guys in the office that I actually liked, but they were not closers. I would cut them a deal by saying, "I don't like to drive. If you take me to the prospect, I'll give you a percentage of the deal if I write it."

Not only did they drive me to the prospect's home, but they sat in on my pitch. It would spin their heads around! Many times they told me, "I can't believe what I just heard!" They said they were impressed watching me close a deal with my Reverse techniques.

Meanwhile, the managers – my immediate bosses – would become intimidated as they watched the salespeople gravitate to me instead of them. It amazed me that the same managers who benefited from my overrides – and it didn't hurt their feelings to accept them – at the same time resented me because of the informal power that I had. The fact is that if these same managers had any talent themselves, those other salespeople would not have been coming up to me for help to begin with.

The intimidation the managers felt went on to become a problem. I never said anything about my production to anybody, but they could see the numbers for themselves. I made it look too easy. The more I built my reputation on being a producer, the more the managers wanted to get rid of me because of their professional jealousy.

One particular company I worked for brought lightweight managers in through the backdoor that shouldn't have been in sales to begin with. These glorified clerks with the title of "manager" weren't as greedy as some other offices I came across, but they were willing to cut off their nose to spite their face by sticking me with a trumped up charge. They fired me because of their egos, and in the process they lost all the money they were making off me. You see, once you let a guy like me go you're overrides are gone as well.

Not every land sales company was as stiff necked as this one. Just two weeks prior, the vice president of the same company had commended me on being the top salesperson. The Reverse was he was one of the people who made the decision to fire me; the other person was my manager. The funny thing is, when my manager was first hired in I had the choice between working under her or another manager.

When I chose her, she was so excited at the time that she threw her arms around me and knocked off my glasses.

"I got Ken George!" she told everyone. She was beside herself. She had come into sales with the illusion that she "was going to help people" as if sales was a sociology class. It's not about helping people, it's about making money. She couldn't make enough money and was a misfit to the job. She resented me because I had informal power with the other salespeople and influence over the office that I didn't even want.

What happened was this: a little school marm who couldn't close a door let alone a sale came to work for the office just after she had gotten her real estate license. They gave her a few leads, one of which I happened to have a copy of. I wrote the deal the next day. When she found out she became very upset, not realizing that her leads were not just unique to her. In all these offices, leads are recycled over and over again. It was very common for 5 or 6 people to have the same lead at the same time.

The school marm told our manager, who was looking for an excuse to fire me anyway. The manager's ego was so fragile she couldn't have a guy like me hanging around.

The manager asked me to defend myself against the accusation. I told her I wasn't even going to dignify a response to such a question. Why would I take someone's leads when I was often splitting deals with the other salespeople? If the little school marm had come up to me personally and told me she had the same lead, I would have given the deal to her. It would have avoided the whole problem. I wasn't going to honor a ludicrous accusation that I "stole" her lead.

When my manager threatened to call the home office, I told her, "Go ahead and call them." She told the general manager who made the call and the vice president told them to fire me.

Leaving that office wasn't a big deal to me. I had already moved to several different offices during the course of my sales career. The nature of the beast was to move to different companies, switching offices to follow the deals wherever they would be. When I left that company the only thing I carried with me was my pen, leaving a wall full of plaques and awards. I wore that firing like a badge of honor.

After walking out, I immediately went up the street to a competitor who had been trying to pirate me for years anyway. When I told them how I was fired, they were in the aisles laughing! They couldn't believe that other company would ever let me go.

At this new company, I was their top salesman for that year and went on to win their national awards.

Later on I met with my attorney and inquired how I could seek damages for being wrongfully terminated.

"You can collect damages only if you lose money," he told me. "You made more at the second company than the first one. They did you a favor. You have no case!"

Isn't that a Reverse?

Meanwhile, within a year the outfit that fired me eventually went belly up and closed their doors. They were once the number one office. It's not that my production alone shut it down, but it was enough to make the difference. The very people that let me go – the general manager and vice president – both were fired themselves for "playing around" with the office secretaries. It was another Reverse! They fired me, and ended up firing themselves.

CAUGHT!

In every office there were head games, which was nothing different for me. I was playing head games even as a kid. I remember sitting upstairs in the movie theater shooting my water pistol with one hand and holding my pea shooter with the other, peppering the audience below. I got a chuckle out of baptizing them before the usher came running up the stairs looking for the perpetrator. When his flashlight landed on me, I Reversed him by pointing to the guys behind me. They were ushered out of the theater yelling "I didn't do anything!" while I continued to spray the audience.

I won that time, but there were moments when I was the one who was Reversed as a mischievous kid. Bear in mind I wasn't exactly Al Capone pulling this off, just your average 10 year old altar boy. One of the few, that is, who had enough respect *not* to sneak a drink of the altar wine.

When I was in school, I would sit at one of the girl's desks and probe around until I found her lunch. I swiped it because I had nothing to eat for myself. It became a habit. Other guys saw me getting away with this and wanted to get in on the action. It wasn't long until lunch thievery became an epidemic. Almost every guy in class was in on my good deal ripping off lunches.

While munching on one of those choice lunches, one of those frustrated black-dressed-penguin nuns started charging down the aisle with her rubber-soled shoe to give a beating to the guy behind me for stealing food out of the desk.

Like a bull on a rampage she passed me wild-eyed while I sniggered, "Get him, get him!" I was already laughing at how this guy was going to get nailed.

Suddenly she did a 180 Reverse and *WHAM!* She nailed me right in the back of the head!

"Keep your hands off those lunches!" she hissed. She beat me senseless. Like the other boys in school, I was just another punching bag for her catharsis. When it was over, I had to thank her for what she had done. After you take a beating, with tears coming down your face because you're so hurt and embarrassed, you'd *better* thank them if you didn't want a repeat performance. At that time you couldn't complain to your parents and have your teacher fired; our parents would applaud them for the beatings they gave us.

I thought I had a home run deal back then. I got caught, but I learned to be efficient and make the most out of what I had, which was nothing. I had to know how to hustle to survive, and learned how to *create something from nothing.* I was hungry so I created a meal. I did it with audacity still knowing that the meal really belonged to some pious little girl.

This is also where I first learned about urgency. I'm hungry *now*, and to avoid the striking blow of some zany nun beating on my head, I learned how to be sneaky and get away with it as much as I could. Sometimes I got caught, and sometimes the other guy would. I took these techniques and used them at various times later on in life in my sales career.

Paraphrasing

Now you understand why I wasn't exactly an amateur at playing head games with these sales offices. It was my stock and trade! They wanted to play, so let the games begin! At every turn some of these low lives were trying to screw me, and I was finding a way to Reverse it.

A great example of this was when I was working at the same land sales office with Sweet Willy. He and a few other bandits were playing ball with the manager to get the leads. They would get the cream of the leads to go out and pitch, and if they didn't score they would "do me a favor" as they said by dumping their recycled garbage leads back on me.

At this time I was still somewhat naïve about receiving help. Later on in my career I didn't want it. Any "help" these managers gave me always had a hook to it. Unbeknownst to me, when the manager gave me a lead it had already been pitched by two or three other salespeople. They wanted to get a good laugh at my expense. When they had mentally given up on it, they would add insult to injury by handing it to me saying, "Here's a fresh lead for you, Ken."

When I went out to pitch these leads, the prospects would stop me before I even got in the door. Some of them were furious. "How many guys are they going to send out here?" they told me. "Tom, Dick, and Harry already came out here from your company. I *don't want* the property."

Discouraged to hear this for several weeks, I thought about how futile it was to chase these dog leads. I was frustrated because I knew that was the only type of lead this organization was going to leave me with. So I had a choice: I could quit or figure out a creative way to Reverse it.

I was giving this some thought when out of nowhere it seemed like a bolt of lightning hit me! If two or three of these guys had already pitched the prospect, they did all the work. *All I had to do was paraphrase…* with a little acting.

When I showed up at the doorstep of the next prospect, he told me the same line I'd been hearing for weeks. "Look, guys keep coming out here and I don't know why you bother. I don't want the property."

I acted surprised, "Who was out here?"

"Dick and Harry were out here——"

"You mean to tell me that Dick was out here at your door? Is he a relative or a close friend or something?"

"No," the prospect said. Now he was curious.

"Well, what were they doing here then?" I asked.

"They were talking about some property."

"What property? Oh, the property on the west coast? They showed you *that* property, and you *passed it up*? Do you realize what you did?"

Now the prospect was concerned. "Wh-what do you mean by that?"

"Look, I don't have much time, I have to leave to make a couple more calls——"

"No, no," he said. "What did you mean by that?"

I said, "I'll tell you what. Let me sit down here and show you something. You have property over here in on the east coast right? And they were showing you inventory here on the west coast? They don't even *show that* at the dinner parties. That was select inventory. If I was you, I'd have put an option on that property ASAP."

"Well what's an option?"

"An option is when you put down a deposit to show good faith. Then you cross your fingers and hope that property is still available. I can tell you right now, what they had that night you may never see again. Anyway, I don't have much time right now."

"Wait, how do I take an option?" the prospect asked.

"Got a pen? Make out your check to the company. I'll get back to you tomorrow if the property is still available. If it's not, I'll return your deposit, but don't get mad at me. Bye."

Of course most of the time I could get the inventory; I was just fudging, playing my role. I'd go back the next day and tell the prospect, "I've got good news and bad news. The good news is you got one. The bad news is somebody else grabbed the second one." I then proceeded to write the deal.

It was a romantic way to sell. If there are any critics who are shocked with this method – *give me a break*. That's why it's called *creative* sales – got it?

When I turned in my contracts at the office, the other salespeople couldn't figure out how I had written deals that they had pitched over and over again to no avail. After they found out I was turning the garbage into gold, they didn't give me any more of their recycled leads. The ones I did write had other salespeople coming out of the woodwork like cockroaches, wanting a piece of the commission because they claimed I wrote their lead.

No matter what they did to me or how it was done, I generally found a way a Reverse to it. If you remember Reader, I mentioned that if somebody is messing with your head, you don't tell them. You never lose until you admit it.

Earlier I pointed out that I fought on two fronts: the office and the prospects. In both arenas, playing head games was essential to survival. What I was doing to the prospects in a pitch, I was also doing to the guys in the office. I'd Reverse the prospect by saying, "I don't know if I can get this for you," and I'd Reverse the office by saying, "Geez, this is must be my lucky night writing that sale." With the prospect, all I had to do was overcome their objections to convince them to buy my product. I was closing 3 out of 5 prospects out of my own leads; the real battle was in the office where the head games with the other salespeople never stopped. The Reverse was I generally won.

Willy also thought he had done a number on me handing me those garbage leads, and I went out paraphrasing exactly what he had said to the prospect with my cute little performance. Generally I wrote 1 out of 5 out of those leads, which Willy considered to be dead.

Those were exciting moments when I could go back to Willy with my numb and dumb act, saying, "I don't know what happened, I guess I got lucky again. That one that you pitched the other night? Boy, they sure were a nice young couple."

"Why?" Willy would ask, suddenly attentive.

"I don't know, but I only wrote them on a couple of lots. They sure liked you, Willy. Thought you were a great guy." I'd really be sticking it to him with that remark. He didn't care if they thought he was a nice guy. He'd rather he wrote the two lots and they thought he was a shark – which he was!

He had gone to a prospect and "put the Willy on them" but couldn't close. When I Reversed him by going back to the same prospect and writing the deal, it blew his cork!

I was at my best when I was doing a number on the office, especially Willy. It was me against the sharks, and I was winning. I think I made those guys more upset by not flaunting my abilities, because that way they couldn't get back at me. I maintained my low profile because I never wanted them to read me. It was said I was a content man.

I had such control over the lightweights in the office that even when I didn't have a plan I still worried them. Whether or not I did, they never knew. I never told them anything either way whether I was up or down. I think I would have been a great actor because the truth was most of the time I didn't have a plan. I wasn't just acting numb and dumb. Of course, they never knew that. I might have been sleeping with my eyes open and they couldn't figure it out. But it made sales fun for me, and it never felt like work.

Playing head games was about not letting on to others what you're capable of. If your competition can read you, they have the upper hand. If they can't, you can keep them guessing while you put them under ether.

The Infamous Ice Cream Incident

In every office I went into, there was a built-in resentment before I even got there. They didn't understand how I could write the volume of deals that I did. They might have thought I was conjuring up deals like Merlin the magician. The more I wrote, the more they resented me.

Because I was such a loner and didn't bother to explain myself, I was a natural target. When you can close, there's a lot of professional jealousy. If I was the same guy, but didn't write any business, then possibly everybody would have viewed me as a great guy because I wouldn't have been a threat. That's a Reverse.

Since I did not have any respect for most of these coffee machine crybabies, they resented my attitude of "in them but not of them." I wouldn't go carousing with these guys at night or drinking down at the bar with them. I would go home and spend time with my family. They didn't like having me around if I wasn't going to be buddy-buddy with them; I was just there to write deals and go home.

I felt like I was giving care packages to my manager and his cronies when I had to give them a piece of my action. These parasites were always trying to pick my pockets with their trumped-up rules. The only thing these lowlife bandits lacked was a gun and a mask. While I was out in the trenches making business, they were in the office with paralysis by analysis. Some managers and lightweight salespeople would bad-mouth me and I treated it like water off a duck's back. They were the blind leading the blind.

One time it was like a lynch mob when the entire office of sales reps came to the door of my office. They were complaining to the general manager.

"How come he doesn't have to come to the meeting?" they cried. "We have to make coffee for the meetings, why doesn't Ken make any of the coffee?"

The general manager came out and told them, "He doesn't go to meetings and he doesn't drink coffee. He just writes deals."

"He just thinks he's better than us!" they said.

The conversation went back and forth until I finally came out of my office.

"Look, you're right," I told them. "I should attend a meeting. But I'll tell you what, I'm not going to attend one today, but I will make the coffee. I'll have it waiting nice and warm for you."

I had never made coffee before in my life. After they had all gone to the meeting room for their weekly rah-rah session, I conjured up my own recipe: yesterday's coffee and tea, mixed with sugar, ketchup, salt, pepper, mustard, and of course some creamer. It was quite a concoction. I heated it up and served it as they came out.

The first guy took a sip and spit it back out. The second guy actually said it was great! He wanted to know what I'd done to make it taste so good, can you believe that? The rest of them didn't like it as much as he did, and said they never wanted me to make the coffee again. That was the end of my coffee debut; I don't think I'm any threat to Starbucks now. The sales reps at that office didn't make an issue of my lack of attendance at their meetings again.

That reminds me of another time I Reversed my opposition. This was back when I was still working as an engineer at one of the major corporations, before I went into sales. I convinced my supervisor that I knew a better way to write my own job description to make the operation more efficient. In essence, what I was doing was convoluting that plan so badly that he never knew what I was doing. However, my job was always completed before I snuck out of the office to go swimming at a nearby island on company time.

I guess I thought nobody could catch me... but eventually some of my nosy coworkers blew the whistle on me. They didn't know I was tipped off about it. The next day, before my boss had a chance to approach me, I stormed into his office with an attitude of incredulity.

I said to my boss, "What are these allegations I'm hearing? You think I went to the island on company time, is that what you're saying? *Are you kidding me*? How would I be able to leave the building, drive all the way down to the island, then come all the way back and still get all my work done?"

"Yes, yes, you're right," my supervisor was flustered. "It's ridiculous, I knew it wasn't true. I shouldn't have bothered you with it." He dismissed the whole thing.

The guys that ratted on me were even more upset that I'd talked my way out of it, but I put up the white flag to them to Reverse them.

"Look, I'll tell you what I'll do for you," I told them. "I'll buy you all double-dip ice cream tomorrow during lunch break to show there are no hard feelings on my part."

Well they didn't really want to be my friends, but they weren't going to say no to free ice cream.

The next day we all walked down several blocks from the office to the store and I bought them ice cream cones. The church bell rang and they all realized they had to get back immediately for a very important meeting that their supervisors were present at. If they weren't on time, they were sure to get it!

They ran up the street, ice cream dripping all over them. Meanwhile, I went around the corner where I strategically parked my car earlier that morning and drove up to the office. As the guys walked in sweaty with ice cream all over themselves, I started banging on the ashtray to get the boss' attention. He came over and caught them all – I had my revenge.

They wanted to play head games with me, and they had lost the match.

On another occasion as a flunky clerk still at the corporation, I couldn't get a raise but I really wanted to buy a convertible. So I started a little cottage industry selling knock-off perfumes in the office. To set it up so I wouldn't get in trouble with the bosses during company time, I greased them first. I'd ask them, "What kinds of perfume does your wife like?" I'd buy off these bosses in order to continue selling my product without their interference.

It was another instance where I created something from nothing. I couldn't earn enough income doing my regular flunky job and the corporation did not offer me any opportunity for extra hours or a raise, I found a creative way to supplement my income. I didn't feel I was taking anything away from the company by using my time this way, considering what some of the other guys were getting away with. Most of the high paid engineers were talking golf scores all day, not completing their jobs on straight time – so they were rewarded with double-time. I had no moral problem with skipping to the beach or hustling perfume on the side.

That year, I bought the convertible.

<u>Revenge is Sweet</u>

Again revisiting the past, as a little kid I was given a dime so I could go to the movies. It was nine cents for the theater and a penny for licorice. At the movies you had a choice of paying nine cents or trading in six wire hangers as a ticket because of a deal the theater had with the cleaners next door. I didn't have the hangers, but I liked that dime. I wasn't going to waste it by paying my way in. By sneaking in I didn't have to end up with just the penny – I got to keep the whole dime. The price was right!

A rat had bit the usher's hand, and it had swollen up to an enormous size. As a little kid, the first thing you see at eye-level is that huge hand hanging down from the usher, taking tickets. He would seem intimidating to any six year old. I walked in to the theater backwards, looking right at him but I was never caught. Week after week I snuck my way in without the infected hand of the usher landing on my shoulder to toss me out. I felt like I was the invisible man.

As I passed the concessions stand I ran my hands through the animated popcorn machines (thus why the theater was called "the bug house") and took a seat to watch the show. The most unique feeling was walking down the aisle to pick a seat and there was a crunch under my feet – I didn't know if it was the popcorn or what had been animating it.

My brother and cousin found out what I was getting away with, and wanted in on the deal. I told them I could sneak them in too, and we could all keep our dimes. I sold them on the idea that it could be done.

The year before when I was five, these same two mischief makers had burst my bubble saying there was no Easter Bunny. As any naïve kid, I was devastated that something I believe in turned out to be a lie. They were having fun at my expense. When they asked me if I could sneak them into the theater, I knew it was my time to show them what *I* could do.

I told my brother and cousin to walk in through the side entrance while I took the door at the front. We all walked in at the same time, and I looked straight at the usher who saw me come in! I pointed over at the side doors and set up my cohorts.

"Hey, those guys are sneaking in!" I said. The usher spun around, and the two guys froze in their tracks. As the usher swooped down to kick them out, I ran my hands through the popcorn machine and then went to find a seat. My diversion had been a success! That's what they got for ruining the Easter Bunny for me. Revenge was sweet.

My brother and cousin had other little scams they were trying to pull on me. I remember as a kid they would talk me into climbing this one apple tree. Then, if it was safe, they would follow after me. This way if the owner of the home whose apple tree we were climbing was to come out, they wouldn't get caught. They could drop down first and escape, leaving me as the sacrificial lamb.

I went up the tree and suddenly the porch light came on. The owner came out and shot a gun into the air. My brother and cousin panicked and dropped out of the tree, running into the alley with the guy chasing them. He hadn't seen me high up in the tree, hiding among the branches. I continued to munch on the apples as I watched them being chased like a *Tom and Jerry* episode.

Instead of becoming the guinea pig for my brother and cousin, they yet again became my decoy. Just as I did with the bug house movie caper, I snatched victory from defeat by creating something from nothing with a Reverse!

I mentioned earlier I used to think I was the invisible man. In my mind, how else could I have gotten away with such mischief as swiping little girl's lunches at school, sneaking into the movies, or climbing up an apple tree and not getting caught? And if I did get caught, I felt I could talk my way out of it with a *mea culpa*.

I'm about creating things, but if people are throwing roadblocks at me I intend not to come in second best, whether it was destroying the image of the Easter bunny in my head or having contempt for my ability in the sales organizations. In each situation I never started the head games first. But I responded to the challenge. They were in my ball pack, and I loved getting revenge back on the people who started it with a Reverse.

I can't forget the time when Willy wrote a deal with a friend of mine using the deception that I would get credit for the sale. Talk about *audacity*! My friend was interested in purchasing a piece of property, but was waiting so I could get him a good offer. In the meantime, Willy came over to his house saying, "Aw yeah, Ken sent me here. We're good friends. He wanted me to make this deal with you."

My friend had no idea that he was lying! When I found out at the office, Willy went through all kinds of gyrations when I approached the general manager about it.

"Aw Ken!" Willy said, "We have to find a way to get through this. I wrote the deal so you need to get over it." I suggested that we flip a coin. He hedged on the offer, getting nervous. The general manager asked me what he was supposed to do about it; the deal was already written.

"Fine, give it to him," I said. "But Willy, you stole this deal from me. I'll get my share of yours!"

When I said that, I didn't present an image of being so numb and dumb anymore. Willy understood I didn't make idle promises. Noting his fragile ego, I said it to him knowing it would make him lose sleep at night. I wanted Willy to know he had been a bad boy, and now it was my duty to put him through redemption for his sins, as I took every opportunity to make my day at his expense.

Eventually, I did take several deals from Willy, just as I promised. Nobody tarnished his ego more than I did. Revenge was sweet.

War Game

Sales is like a war game. There's a winner and a loser, and I never lose. The only other venue I can think of that can teach somebody reality is if you actually went to war. When you're in the trenches there, at least you have a weapon to shoot back with. In sales, when you go in the trenches, you have no weapons. You have to outwit the prospect without fighting back directly. If not, you lose.

Getting back to my friend Willy, as I said he would often intimidate the neophytes by flashing around the contracts he had written. A lot of these salespeople quit because they couldn't handle Willy's head games. His logic was that if there were less salespeople that meant more leads for him and less competition. He didn't understand how he couldn't get his head games to work on me too.

I never told him that I knew he was putting on an act – that was the beauty of it! Willy could never accept how I could produce as much business as I did with those recycled garbage leads. But I got from him what I wanted from everybody: *respect*.

Willy would say in his whining tone, "*Nyeh*, I heard of your presentations. They could use a little polish. *Nyeh*, if I could help you any way…"

I said, "No, I've seen the way you helped those other guys you broomed out of here."

I was always pretending I didn't hear what he was saying about me, like it didn't penetrate me, but I heard every word. He knew I was just putting on an act pretending how lucky

I was falling into all these deals, but I was always playing myself down.

I'd still come in every morning dressed in my T-shirt and sandals to bring my contracts into the office. Other salespeople with three-piece suits and attaché cases sat around the office, staring at me with an incredulous look, thinking, *how does Ken do it?* I was still playing the role of the stupid bumpkin to them, scratching my head as I dumped the contracts on the receptionist's desk. Willy was especially aware of the volume of sales I was writing.

My mind was always active, thinking of ways to Reverse Willy with the same head games he was using on everyone else. Once I remembered I'd made a mistake on one of the contracts I wrote. I went back to the receptionist, asking her to check out the contract where I'd left a line open. She said, "You write too many contracts! We'll never find which one it was."

What a nice problem to have! I went back to my office, scratching my head for effect while the other salespeople stared at me with a look of awe.

"I'm a lucky guy, I guess," I would say. "These deals are just falling in my lap."

I continued that mystique. No matter what office I went to, they generally already had an opinion of me because the word went out about my reputation. They knew I could write a lot of business and made some of the other salespeople look bad, causing a lot of professional jealousy. Many of them couldn't write a deal if it came up and bit them in the hand.

I always made it a point after writing one of Willy's garbage leads to thank him. I would say, "Nobody else gave me a lead this week, thank you Willy." I acted like I didn't realize that this recycled lead was something he couldn't write himself. He was sticking it to me just to be obnoxious, and I was Reversing him.

It was the same tactic I was using against the King Kong attitude of some of the prospects who were beating their chests, asserting "I'm the decision maker in this house." I would immediately tell them with a Reverse that they were more of an expert than I am on the product that I was pitching. I'm sure the prospect spent time before the appointment telling his wife how he was "going to deal with me," but I have already disarmed him so that he doesn't get the opportunity to unload on me.

I found more ways to upset the prospect's apple cart by what I *didn't* say, or maybe a funny look I gave them. I maintained my dignity by not letting the prospect have an opportunity to bad mouth me and make me feel negative about myself. If I didn't make the sale, I made sure in a diplomatic way that he was going to suffer the loss – not me.

Possibly I'd say, "What you just passed on, you may never see this opportunity again. But have a nice day because maybe you couldn't afford it anyway,"

That's a little zinger when you tell the prospect they can't afford something. I'd say it slow and sure, and shake his hand as I did it. He couldn't get back at me because I was being friendly at the same time I was zinging him. It's more frustrating for him. When you do that, you at least come out a winner by maintaining your dignity.

Some prospects could afford to lose because they could go back to their 9-to-5 jobs to support their family. I didn't have the luxury of losing – sales was my occupation. I paid the price to pay the bills to support my own family. They thought they were going to stick it to me, but I wouldn't give the prospect a chance. I had to maintain my own momentum. As I said, it was a war.

How could anyone be in the sales business and not be strong? How do they justify to their family that they had the right to sit around all day smoking and sucking up coffee in the office, knowing they weren't going to be able to pay their bills and let their family suffer? How could they justify that? I could never, just as I couldn't understand how others at my early flunky clerk's job could come in on overtime because they didn't perform their jobs on regular time while they were talking about baseball scores.

After my layoff from the corporation, I was out in the street with three kids to support. I entered sales only to pay the bills, I didn't have any aspirations to go beyond that. But my nemesis Willy screwing me out of the first contest was the game changing moment of my life that gave me the motivation to become the "ace of aces," as they called me. I didn't want to play head games, but if Willy or the other salespeople were going to play them with me, then it was on.

It's tough for the average salesperson to survive in the creative sales environment because they soon realize that they really are in shark infested waters. When everyone is stealing from you and getting into your pocket, you generally don't want to hang around them.

I saw it the other way – I knew that a lot of them were con men. My own manager was working in competition against me! That's what I was up against. The Reverse was, instead of destroying me, it forced me to be even more creative.

That's why I could play Willy. I knew what a cunning guy he was with all these traps he would lay for me and the other salespeople. He would take me out to lunch, sitting right next to me with that routine he had like he was indifferent about sales and so concerned about my health and my kids, and that he wanted me to be successful. Yeah, *right*.

"*Nyeh*, can I help you in any way Ken?" he continually asked me.

"Boy that's awfully decent of you Willy." I would really be thinking, *Just eat your pie.*

That's when he'd sneak some questions in while sipping on his coffee. "Oh and by the way Ken, that last deal you pitched, I pitched those people too. How come they didn't – not that it matters – but how come I didn't close them and you did?"

"I don't know Willy," I would say. "Oh, this coffee's cold! Take it back." – I would break up the conversation while he's focused on me, trying to squeeze any information he can out of me – "All I did was go back after you pitched them and said what you said. When is that food going to come out?"

Willy *knows* he's trying to con me and I'm conning him right back. It was like two nitwits playing stupid when both of us were very smart at what we were doing, but we never let on to each other. He knew that I must know something to take away a deal that he already pitched and couldn't close.

Anyway, I was getting a free meal out of the guy while he was trying to pump me.

When we went back to the office and making small talk, there'd be a line of salespeople at the door listening in on us. They were tuned in because they wanted to know what trade secrets we were talking about. We talked about a whole lot of nothing! Everything we touched or said has a Midas Touch and instantly gained value in the eyes of the other salespeople. It was really worthless – that was the point! But I gave the image that there *was* something to it.

We were the talk of the whole division in the company. "Really, who's the best: Willy or Ken?" they would say. I knew I didn't need him, but at times he needed me. It didn't matter, and if it did I wouldn't tell him. Just like the other salespeople in the office, I told him a whole lot of nothing. I didn't particularly want to help him because he was doing well on his own before I came along. So when he asked me specifically about my presentations, I told him the truth. It was my ploy; he didn't believe I was laying it right in his lap!

Willy's must have been thinking, *He can't be telling me everything. It can't be the truth.*

But it was! That was the Reverse!

I pulled that on everybody. I told them everything I was doing, just the way I did it. But I'd have that silly smile on my face that gave them that doubt. I never made them feel secure.

These thieves were stealing from me what I would have gladly given to them for nothing! I didn't respect them and I didn't want to be part of them. I would not let them have any part of me. But you have to play ball once in a while or they'll find a way to trip you up. I didn't because I was a master at playing head games.

At times I would talk about a whole lot of nothing. Other times when they asked – as Willy would – I told them exactly how I used my techniques, but they couldn't accept it as the truth because it was something they seldom used. Thus, the greatest Reverse is the truth.

Emotion vs. Logic

When I came to the door, many prospects may have thought to themselves, "I can handle this salesman because I'm a logical person." What they didn't know was that I disarmed them with emotion.

Allow me to give you an example of control during a pitch with a presentation I made to a pipe smoking engineer who made an inquiry:

As usual I was dressed with my usual T-shirt and sandals, playing my humble role. I didn't have an attaché case or the typical three-piece suit like most other salespeople. The only thing I carried was a brochure in my hand and a pen in my pocket. When I came to the door this way I wanted to give the prospect the edge and let him think he was the one in control. After all, I was on his turf and he'd surely want to impress his wife with his logic to make himself look good at my expense.

I asked the prospect, "Are you the decision maker in this family?"

"Of course I am," the engineer said, with the tone of King Kong beating on his chest. He turned and told his wife, "I'll take care of this honey. Get back in the kitchen."

Once I was inside, he told me, "Wipe your feet. Sit down over there, we haven't finished our meal yet." I sat in the chair and hunkered down, making myself look tiny and insignificant. When he finished his dinner and came back into the living room burping, he said, "Now what's this all about?"

"Mr. Jones," I said, "I want to tell you up front, I'm not an expert on this product. You probably know more about it than I do."

Why did I say this? Well, what if he *did* know more about what I was promoting than I did? It disarmed him from using that knowledge as ammunition against me. He couldn't ambush me that way because I've already admitted he's the expert, not me.

During the presentation I asked Mr. Jones, "What if I could offer you the best quality, does that mean anything to you?" I waited for a positive response. Once he said yes, I went on. He just made a commitment. If he hadn't said yes, I would have kept asking or rephrasing the question until I got it out of him. Without closing the commitment, I never went on to the next one.

The next question I asked was, "What if I could offer you the best service, does that mean anything to you?" Once he committed, then I'd ask, "And what if I could also offer you the best price, does that mean anything to you?"

If I didn't get these commitments from the prospect, I would stop the presentation. Every one of these commitments had to be yes because they trapped the prospect to either buy or lie at the close. If they don't make the commitment to every proposition, the prospect will cop out at the close.

Now that the prospect has agreed to all of my proposals, I took out one of those basic brochures about the property he had asked about in the lead I had. In seconds I could lead him to what he wanted to buy, but never quite let him have it. I would keep him a little off balance by Reversing him to another product, and as soon as he thinks he's got me figured out, I'd again Reverse him again to another product. After all this mental surgery, in the end I brought him back to his original choice, but only after he understood that I had control and he didn't.

Now that the engineer thought he was firmly in control, I had to qualify and see if he was the real decision maker in the family he claimed he was.

In my seminars I often ask who the decision maker was in such a presentation. Some say the husband, some say the wife, and some say both of them. Ready for the real answer? The only decision maker is *the salesperson*. I'll ultimately let Mr. Jones *think* he is the decision maker in order to keep his ego from being shattered at the close.

But first, in order to set up my credibility, I said, "Did you attend any of my seminars? Are you sure I didn't see you there? Well, at these seminars I would evaluate your investments similar to a financial planner. For example, asking what you invest in – stocks, bonds?"

As I said this, I repeatedly looked down at my watch. I didn't want to give him the impression I was anxious to sell him anything. My Reverse on the prospect is that I don't have much time and must leave. I started tapping my pen on the desk, and got up to put my coat on. Just like a good comedian's joke, it's all about the rhythm and timing of how you play the game. It's done so quickly that the prospect – who was proud that he could be so tight lipped about his financial situation – was now getting diarrhea of the mouth trying to impress me with his investments.

Now that I've qualified the alleged decision maker, I went down the roster of what he's told me, complimenting him on almost every investment… *except for one.* I wanted him to take the money out of his weakest investment and put it in *my* investment. Again I used mental surgery to open up his mind. By securing his commitments and knocking out his objections with third person stories, I had him somewhat controlled, and he knew it. I've negated his logic with emotions, something he wasn't prepared for. Of course, I had to do it with tact so that he didn't rebel by closing his wallet.

Now is when Mr. Jones came up with objections as to why he wasn't interested. There are only 5 or 6 obvious objections. "I can't afford it… I don't buy what I can't see… I know a better deal somewhere else… I'll drive down to see it myself… I want to think about it…" and on.

Before he can hit me with these objections, I've already used third person stories to show him how ludicrous they were, so he can't use them. Before the prospect can tell me he's going to drive all the way to see the property for himself before he buys, I tell him, "Can you believe Mr. Jones, I had a friend of mine in sales who had a client – get *this!* Here's a guy with a couple kids who's going to drive a thousand miles on a vacation – spend all that time with those kids screaming in the back seat – and then drive another couple hundred miles, hoping to find this lot sitting way out in the boondocks. And he expects to come all the way back and tell the salesman if he wanted to buy it or not. I mean, he couldn't even tell what the soil percolation was, and he's going to make a decision like he's a real estate expert? Can you believe that?"

While I said this, I checked to see if he was sweating or his cheeks were flushed. I wanted to see if he was getting too stressed out. If I thought that I was putting on too much subtle pressure, I might do something like drop my pen or look out the window. "Looks like rain!" I would say, which eases the pressure of the situation. It relaxes the prospect. And when he's totally off guard, I go for the jugular and close by saying, "Got a pen? Okay, make out your check to the Company."

9 out of 10 people were animated to their checkbook by the question, "got a pen?" Even though I've got several of my own in my pocket, I'm moving him towards the close.

Now this American Hero, who is "in control" on his own turf because he's supposedly the decision maker in the family, will almost always invariably turn to his wife and say, "what do you think, honey?" If he is saying "yes, sir" all day long to his boss and "yes, honey" all night to his wife, he is definitely *not* the decision maker.

Once I sensed resistance by Mr. Jones, I took the opportunity to divide and conquer with a Reverse by complimenting *Mrs.* Jones. I asked her, "Who bought this house? I bet it was your idea, wasn't it Mrs. Jones?"

"Yes, see I told you it was a good idea honey," she gloated over her husband. I now have an ally.

I turned my attention back to Mr. Jones. "You have to understand this property isn't a question of if you want it – it's *if* you can get it."

I Reversed him again! I continued, "So if you both have come to the conclusion that you want this property if the inventory is available, I'll have to check it with my home office. If it's there, you got a deal. If it's not, don't get mad at me.

What do you think about this technique? He was sitting in his castle, saying "I'm logical" but I've broken him down emotionally. Finally I said to him, with the checkbook in front of me, "Do you want it in both of your names?"

Now they've signed the deal.

Knowing from experience that almost every fifth deal will cancel the next day, I held the contract up to the couple after they've signed it and asked them, "Do you intend to cancel this? If you are, tell me now and I'll tear it up."

Only *once* in my career did I ever have to tear a contract. Some salespeople were shocked by the audacity of this question, and asked why I would tear it up and lose the deal. The truth is the prospect would have just canceled the next day anyway, so it didn't matter. If the contract is torn, I've eliminated it from my mind so I can move on to the next prospect up the street.

Once the prospect and his wife have assured me they won't cancel, I make sure they *thank me*. I won't thank them. If I thank them, I'm a peddler. If they thank me, I'm a professional. I never said thank you to a prospect after selling them a deal.

Reader, I can hear some of you saying right now, "That isn't very polite." Well I wasn't trying to be rude. In fact, usually the prospect were so happy with the deal they were thanking me anyways, not the other way around. That's a Reverse; you have to be able to delineate the difference between Emily Post's "proper etiquette" and what are just plain good manners.

As Mr. and Mrs. Jones are thanking me, I said "Look, if you want to make it up to me, you can take me out to dinner sometime..."

I ate very well. I was pushing the envelope with audacity. Can you understand that, Reader? The prospect just bought my deal, and on top of it I'm allowing him to buy me a dinner. Now that's control with a Reverse!

Though it may or may not be the proper thing to say to a prospect, it's was a whole lot different than sucking up to them like a beggar going for scraps. I've seen some of these pitchmen coming in kissing the babies and petting the dog, getting buddy-buddy with the prospect with compliments and blowing hot air. If they wrote the deal, they'd go back to the office – or the local waterhole – and brag about how they "took down some sucker." I generally was grateful to any prospect for any deal that I wrote, which was a Reverse from these types of guys.

The prospects were not fools. Some of them understood my audacity during the pitch, and knew my method was generally unorthodox... *they got it*. It was impressive for them to see a salesperson who didn't suck up to them. They understood that I didn't live or die by any deal.

For the record, I never received a single cancellation from a prospect for not saying "thank you."

Oh yeah, there's a good chance I won't thank you for buying this book either.

The Academy Award

Instead of salespeople using their time to seek out new prospects, they should find a reason to go back to the prospects they've already sold. The Reverse is most salespeople figure it's not worth it, so they avoid the prospects they've already sold. I've seen this in every field of sales I worked in. Most salespeople don't try to get back in because they don't realize the power of this golden opportunity. You never know when a prospect can offer you a referral or you can resell them again.

So how do you get another sale out of a prospect that's already been sold? If you saw it in a movie, you'd think I was performing magic as a sat across the table from some of these prospects. It was an Academy Award performance. The lead actor approaches the front door of the prospect, and the stage is set. Let's take a look at the script...

Prospect: "What's this all about?"

Me: "Quite frankly I'm not sure. You bought some property with the company awhile back. The office asked me to come by and review your paperwork because there was a computer glitch at the office."

The prospect hands me his paperwork and I start to look over his information, which is just my excuse to get in the door.

Me: "Oh...uh-oh...."

Prospect: "What's wrong?"

Me: "You bought property over on the east coast?"

Prospect: "Yeah, what about it?"

Me: "Nothing." I sighed.

Prospect: "What do you mean nothing?"

Me: (looking at my watch) "Look, I don't have much time, I have to get back to the office on another call."

Prospect: "Well, what did you mean by that?"

Me: "Have you ever attended my seminars?"

Prospect: "What seminar?"

Me: "We used to go over people's portfolios at the seminar and review what was good, what was bad... let me see, you use a middle initial in your name?"

I broke the rhythm of our conversation because I did not want to react too quickly to his questions. I went back to the nonsense of paperwork which meant nothing.

Me: "Your wife's name... let me see... the lot number, is that your correct lot number?"

Prospect: "W-w-wait a minute, what about this seminar, what are you saying?"

Me: "Look, I've got to get this right, the office is very serious about this paperwork... where's my coat?"

Prospect: "W-wait, what were you going to tell me about...?"

Me: *lowering my voice* "Look, I don't have much time,
            I'll just tell you this: I noticed you were over
            here on the east coast. Did you hear about the
            inventory they're releasing on the other side of
            the coast?"

Prospect: "No."

Me: "Oh, you didn't attend my seminar, that's right.
            I'll tell you what we do. It's going to be the latest
            thing when this property on the other side breaks
            loose. It's not a question of if you want it; it's a
            question of if you can get it. Quite frankly, I don't
            know if you have any pull with the company…"

Prospect: "What do you mean I don't have any pull?"

I brought out a map of the properties and pointed to
the east coast.

Me: "See this stuff over here where you bought your
            property? That's where the money is. The land on
            the west coast is good property for living, not for
            investing like the property you have right here.
            Quite frankly what we did at the seminars we'd go
            over your portfolio and ask people what did you
            have, your home, your stocks and bonds? What's
            your portfolio? I see you have your house."

Prospect: "Yeah, I own my house."

Me: "Any stocks, bonds?"

Prospect: "Yes, I have some stocks."

Me: "Any mutual bonds?"

Prospect: "Yeah, I'm not too happy with them."

Me: "Yeah, I understand what you mean there. Quite frankly, with the house, I don't know who made that decision, but that's a winner. Stocks and bonds are long-term; they're a safe bet when you've got the government protecting you. But the mutuals? *I don't know.* You know what we used to tell the people at the seminars, if you had mutual stocks?"

Prospect: "What?"

Me: "Go out and take a trip. Have a party! You might as well use the money because you're probably losing your butt on that one. However, when people ask me what I would do, I would leverage this property. I'd take that mutual fund – not all of it, it'll come back – I'd take just 10% - and play leverage with it."

Prospect: "What's leverage?"

Me: "Simply this: you invest the least amount to control a larger investment over a longer period of time as it goes up in value. I would suggest taking 10% from the mutuals and put it down on the property, and leave the other 90% where it is where it will hopefully grow. If it does you've got just 10% controlling the property, and if the value of the mutual stock goes up as well you've got both investments increasing in value with the same money that was just sitting in your mutual––but I don't have any time right now. Here's what I can do for you, if you've got some money now

I'll take an option and see if there's any available. If not, the option will be returned to you."

Prospect: "Oh, I'd appreciate it. Thank you!"

I wasn't a lowly peddler anymore in his eyes. By this point, I had his respect.

Me: "I didn't mention it, but I handle the special allocations inventory at the office. If I call you and can pull this off, great. If I don't, don't get mad at me. I'll check with you tomorrow night. If we have a deal, you can thank me then and buy me dinner."

I closed the sale and also got a free dinner out of it… as well as came back again for referrals. Not bad, huh? Of course I made the property look hard to get – that is what creative sales is. You romance the property – it's no different than any other product or service that is being promoted, so lighten up critics.

Sometimes the best pitch is the shortest pitch. Let me give you a quick example: I once went to this fellow's house and he was talking with his buddy on the phone.

I said, "I was sent here by the office to check the inventory of the property you bought previously with us."

"I'm busy now, I can't talk to you," he waved me off.

I said, "Well, it will only take a minute."

He began to get annoyed. "I told you I'm busy," he said.

I shrugged my shoulders and said, "Hey no problem, I'd rather be playing golf, I guess some people can't afford to make any money."

He stopped when he heard that. Apparently I had hit his button because he said, "What did you mean by that?"

I said, "There's some inventory coming in on the other side of the coast. This stuff isn't offered at the normal sales parties, you have to know somebody to get it. And I understand some of that inventory just broke loose, but it's possible to get it through an option."

"What do you mean an option?" he asked. Now he was really interested.

I told him, "If you take an option and if it comes in – cross your fingers – you've got yourself the property. If not, forget about it. I don't want you getting mad at me."

He called into the house, "Honey, bring the checkbook out here." I took the option and next day I wrote the deal.

Like I said, the shortest pitch can be the best pitch. This is especially true when selling to a professional such as a doctor. You have little time with them because they have patients in their office that they have to take care of. A doctor is the only type of prospect you can pitch by themselves. You don't need their spouse with them because they generally make decisions without their spouse's approval.

One doctor I sold to was running back and forth between patients in different rooms. He came in to see me and asked with a rush, "Whatdya got?"

I said with an assumptive attitude, "Doc, here's what we're going to do. We're going to take the money that's probably in some dead-end investment, and I'm going to put it to control the property of these condominiums on the golf course. Also, I'll get back to you if there's any more on the market. For now we're going to go with this. Make out your check to the company for the down payment. And give me back my pen when you're done. I lose more pens that way to you guys."

You guys?! I'm saying this right to a doctor's face! He wrote the check and I wrote the deal. That was it!

The doctor bought because the golf course property was hard to get – making it invaluable – but also because of the pure audacity I had to talk big numbers to him. It impressed him. In my experience, it's much easier to take $50,000 from a doctor than $5000 from Joe Lunchbucket. The hardest pitches I ever made were to Joe Lunchbuckets because that small amount of money was all they had.

Closing the Ego

In sales, the first person you have to sell is yourself. Once I was sold on an idea I could generally sell it to the prospect. It had to be done tactfully with a gradual mental surgery, in order to open the prospect's mind to the sale. With control, you can start at any almost point in a pitch. It keeps the prospect off balance and out of control, not knowing where you're coming from because now they can't predict your next move.

If you're a closer, you'll many times have to play yourself down. Your aptitude hasn't changed, just your attitude. If you ask the prospect a question, you're putting them on the spot. It's a Reverse from them asking you questions. I would at times tell the prospect, "Instead of telling me all the reasons why you don't want this product, tell me one reason why you should. Make it good, I'll write it down."

I met a lot of salespeople who were good closers, but had an issue with honesty. I was honest with prospects. The conman could never do what I did because they lied and cheated whenever they could get away with it. If you're a thief, you're going to project it. You could smell it on them.

Generally the prospects that I dealt with that had 9-to-5 jobs initially acted like I was just another peddler coming up to their door. They didn't look past their noses to think that salesmen like me are the reason they might have a job. At their jobs the prospects could make certain products, but who's going to buy them if you don't have someone selling them? Salespeople sell what is produced indirectly keeping prospects employed – another Reverse.

Many prospects had tender egos, trying to look good in front of their spouses as they went head-on with me over a sale. If I shredded that ego too much, I would cost myself a sale. You have to know when to give them a victory. For example, I would congratulate them at the end of the sale. I'm commending the guy, shaking his hand before he goes to strut in front of his wife. He must have been thinking, "Wait a minute…what happened here?!"

I once sat for 8 hours one time in a prospect's home to write a deal. He called the home office and complained that I had kept him and his family from eating dinner, and cancelled the deal. He was upset because I fractured his ego and beat him. He wrote a nasty letter to the home office of the company about the pressure I put on him during the pitch.

Sometime later I saw *the same guy* at the company in one of the sales training classes because he wanted to learn how to do the same thing! How's *that* for a Reverse?

Many times I would get to the close, look at the prospect and tap my pen on the desk and say, "Got a pen?" The prospect would get up and go to find a pen! I'm animating him to the checkbook, and thus to the close. Once the pen is in his hand, I say, "Fine, make out your check to the company."

At one time, a prospect stopped halfway through writing his signature on his check when he said, "Hey wait a minute! I don't know if I want this!"

"You're probably right, you can't handle this property anyway," I agreed with him.

"Well now, w-wait a minute――"

They would either buy or lie to get out of the pressure. I had to be careful and play back all of their commitments I got during the pitch.

Here's a lesson to some of the long-winded sales types who like to flatter their egos with all the product knowledge they acquire in those rah-rah sales classes. The prospect is just being courteous by listening. Their first priority is to put up a defense mechanism called objections, to overcome the good deal you're offering to them. Remember, they have heard it all before. As I stated earlier, the best pitch is the shortest pitch. I pointed out in an earlier chapter why you don't want to fall in the same trap that salespeople generally do. I suggest the Reverse – instead of you spinning all the smoke and mirrors about how you're an expert, tell the prospect that *they* are the expert. This will not only flatter this ego, but disarm them from using objections against you when you use third-person stories.

Let me explain this in simple terms; you can't guarantee that the prospect does or doesn't know anything about the product or service you're offering. And if they do, do you really want to go toe-to-toe with them on it, with an argument? You may win the battle, but you'll lose the war when the prospect closes their wallet and shows you the door. Not only that, if you *do* challenge the prospect, they've put you in the position to defend. You never want to defend, it's suspect. It's much wiser to agree (a Reverse). Once you've agreed, the prospect is disarmed because they can't clobber you with all their ammunition of objections.

Often times the prospect *wants* the property I'm trying to sell them, but they're so insecure they try to find a way out of the deal. At times they're using levity as a way to laugh their way out of buying, but I didn't give them any way out. I used their objections and commitments as ammunition against them.

When a prospect came up with a ridiculous objection – such as there being swampland or alligators on the property I was going to sell them – I wouldn't defend myself. I would agree with them by saying, "They're free when you buy the property." Then I'd continue with the pitch. I didn't dwell on their ignorant objections. There never was any swampland or gators on any property that I ever promoted.

Most importantly, I didn't defend against the prospect's objections. To defend is suspect. Here's the formula: agree – disarm – attack (and in that order). This is what I refer to as "mental surgery." You knock out his objections with third-person stories, slowly but surely using their own commitments at the close. That's control.

I've been asked in my past seminars why I didn't use the *first*-person (*I, me, you*) to counter the prospect's objections. Why? Because you could not get away with ridiculing their objections to their face. They could feel insulted. By using third-person (*he, she, they*), you're making someone else the heavy, not you. You hit the prospect with a counter to their objection before they can use it on you first. What could they possibly do for an encore? Do you get it?

It's been my experience that if you ever give the prospect a loophole, they'll find a way to cop out with it. If I told the prospect that the land they want is readily available, they would generally find a way to procrastinate, wanting more time to "think about it." I never set myself up for that. I would always say "*if.*" I guaranteed nothing. I was always shifting gears so the prospect didn't know what to expect. This is how I maintained control – which is what the Reverse is all about.

If you buy all of the prospect's cop out rejections, he'll mess up your head. He will have *sold YOU* on the idea that he didn't want it. You take that rejection and accumulate it with all the others you'll end your sales career. Pretty soon you won't want to get out of bed in the morning. To maintain my momentum, I preferred a win-win. I will always win, whether I made the sale or I didn't. Remember that I used the prospect's commitments, not mine. They could only can buy or lie.

Who's lying, you ask Reader? How about when the prospect said they would drive down to the property on their way on their vacation. They didn't. They told me they couldn't afford the deal, yet they said they're well off. They told me they would buy it, then canceled. The prospect told me he was the decision maker, and then he defers to the wife. So who's doing the lying here? These are their commitments that trap the prospect in the lie. If anybody's being dishonest here, it's the guy across the table.

When prospects wimped out they would many times lie to me! I pretended I didn't hear them. But it was registered there, and I savored it when I needed it as a weapon. I only repeated their own commitments and shot it back at them. I didn't have to do anything else. That's what control can do for you. And with this Reverse I had them under ether to the point that every time they thought they knew where I was going with my next statement, I'd shift gears again. I did not want them to feel any confidence whatsoever until the mental surgery was over which prepared them for the final close.

If you really want to understand how to use the Reverse in a pitch, call me at 586-873-2987 to attend my next seminar, or for a personal consultation.

Just like with the salespeople in the office, I was playing head games with the prospect. During the pitch I would use a combination of facial expressions, omissions, and commissions. Sometimes the most effective closing was a stare with just a grunt, or lack thereof.

I would ask the prospect politely, "Did you understand what I just said? Could you please repeat it to me?" If they could, I knew they were listening. If they couldn't, I would repeat it again. I wanted them to know exactly what I said so I could get their commitments that were necessary at the close.

Many times I was anticlimactic, pretending I was leaving in order to disarm the prospect. It was the Colombo Effect. Colombo was a guy who wore a shabby raincoat in a 1970s detective TV show. He was always going, but he never left. I would walk towards the door, telling the prospect that I'd call them the next day after I'd checked the inventory of the property, when halfway out the door I would say, "Oh, wait a minute. Let me check on the phone with allocations right now. Cross your fingers."

I looked over at the prospect as I've got the phone in my hand, asking the office secretary, "Is the inventory from Willy's cancellation still available over there? Did he peddle it yet? No, there's one left?"

I put my hand over the receiver, and told the prospect, "I've got good news for you, Willy didn't peddle it. Hold on, how do you spell your last name?"

Now I know this is an old sales technique, but usually was still effective. In the next moment I was talking into the phone again saying, "Yeah, this lot is for Mr. Smith's family. We're doing the contract right now. Bye bye." I hung up the phone and told the prospect, "Make out your check to the company."

What I'm explaining to them is so quick that all the movements, the hand signals, the silences, everything I'm saying to the prospect comes down to this: when greed exceeds skepticism, the prospect will buy. They say too much knowledge is a dangerous thing, and if that's true, then who among us has nothing to fear? Don't try to impress a prospect with all of your knowledge, because they're not buying the product, they're buying you. The product/service becomes the byproduct, and you become the sale.

One more thing: don't get sold by the prospect's objections. If you don't close the prospect, they may in turn have closed *you* on the idea that they can't be sold. Now that's a Reverse.

Pay attention sales types! Sales is like acting out a performance to the prospect. If you still think you haven't learned anything, just think about this: I closed you when you bought this book. It's a far cheaper education than going to Harvard. You're learning already.

Pipeline to Profits

If salespeople were struggling pitching face-to-face with the prospect, can you imagine how intimidated they would get trying to use the phone? Even the best closers in the business are gun-shy pitching prospects with Mr. Bell's device. Most salespeople were intimidated by it, but I *loved* it. I believed the phone could be one of the best tools to make a deal. I can't explain why I was so comfortable using it. Most of the time I was able to immediately draw a conceptual framework of the type of person I was pitching just by hearing their voice over the phone. It was not ESP, but it must have been the next thing to it.

When you're on the phone, you have to anticipate everything the prospect will say. You have to be able to target their hot button immediately, and qualify them. Once I had their financial information, I knew what investment was the weakest one to attack because I needed that money to be transferred into buying my product.

There were naysayers who said it wasn't possible for me to find out the prospect's investments over the phone – who would give up their financial information to a stranger? But I had it out of them in minutes. Think about that – would you tell a stranger over the phone how much money you have? I'm not talking about stupid people; they could be doctors or lawyers – they would be the first to tell you that nobody was going to get that information out of them. I was fast and to the point so that I got it out of them immediately. Why? Because I knew I was just a click away from them hanging up on me.

There was a time when these hotshot closers from New York would come down to meet me. They said, "I heard about this guy who thinks he can qualify people's incomes over the phone. I don't believe it. He could never do that in New York."

Of course I would agree with them (remember the formula: agree, disarm, then attack). I would go along with them… and then proceeded to show them exactly how I got this information. They were shaking their heads the whole time. They continued their negative naysayer attitude, but at the same time they were taping me! They wanted to learn how to do it too, isn't that a Reverse?

I would think, *Hey dumbbell, you can tape me word for word but you'll never be able to do it.*

Along that line, there was another occasion when a salesman came out of town and I gave him a ride in my car. As I answered his questions about how I pitched, I kept hearing this clicking noise. When I came to a red light, I realized it was the sound of a tape recorder which the guy had covered up under his coat.

I said, "You didn't have to operate a Watergate here, I would have given you this information for nothing."

Just like Willy, these guys were always trying to pump me, not realizing that they didn't need to be sneaky about it.

Here is what they wanted to know: In my opinion, the phone is a technique of *time, timing,* and *tone.* You have seconds to connect with the prospect. You have to create an image of control to a voice that does not see you or even know you. I wouldn't suck up or drop names in my presentation. If nothing else, I quickly painted a picture that made the prospect curious enough to listen to my short, punchy pitch.

When I made an appointment on the telephone with a prospect, I'd say the obvious and at times he wouldn't even know he'd been pitched. For example, I'd say, "If this inventory comes in, it's not question of if you want it, it's a question of if you can get it. If you pass it up, you may never see it again. I can come over at six or seven, what's better for you? Six? Fine. I don't want you getting mad at me if I can't pull this off. When I come over you tell me yes or you tell me no. See you then, bye."

I'm not afraid to ask the question every salespeople is afraid of: tell me yes or tell me no. That's audacity! I didn't want to hear any hedging from the prospect. I already knew how I was going to box them in with their own commitments so they would usually have to say yes. I don't like *no*, but if the prospect doesn't buy he's not going to have his ego intact when I get off that phone. He will suffer a loss because I would always win. Remember Reader, losing was a luxury I could not afford.

Either way as I've said, I didn't personally live or die whether I wrote a deal or not. I've seen skim-scam artists hoodwink prospects over the phone, but they were not comfortable with it and generally had a weak batting average. Were you paying attention Reader when I told you the shortest pitch is the best pitch? With an assumptive attitude this can work over the phone as well as in front of a prospect. When greed exceeds skepticism, you've got a done deal. Greed is not the only motivation a prospect may be driven by when he buys; it could be love and affection. But if it was greed, they bought. As Aristotle said, "*The avarice of mankind is insatiable.*"

On the phone it may look like I was doing an hour a day of real work, but there was so much more that went into analyzing how I got to the close. Until I thought about it years later, *How was I able to predict that with a certain rhythmic presentation I would close the sale?* I'm not sure I knew how valuable my technique really was. To me it was a strong conversation. But I suspect every word I said on the phone was closing them. So when I'm training other salespeople I can tell them – in the door or over the phone – why I was able to make that sale.

Remember even thought I went to the local prospect's door, 30% of the time the entire sale took place over the phone, sight unseen, as I was selling them property a thousand miles away. The prospects had not seen me or the property and still I was able to sell to them for years.

I heard over and over from prospects, "You would never sell me a pig in a poke. I don't buy anything before I can see it."

I would say, "I understand, I'm not selling pigs anyway. Do you buy insurance? Isn't that sight unseen?"

With just a few words over the phone, I generally knew that I could write the prospect before I'd even seen them. Because I was able to bring in business without even leaving the office, the other salespeople in the office were actually complaining I was going through the recycled leads too fast! I caught a lot of heat over that, can you believe it? I wasn't given new leads; these were leads that had been pitched already by the same salespeople who were now complaining because I was writing deals with them.

Many sales types are stuck on details like mail outs to prospects, trying to get a lead. Personally, it's a cop out because many of them have the fear of intimidation to face prospects, so they rationalize they are busy doing something productive. Personally, as a Reverse, I simply pick up the phone.

Instead of wasting my time with flyers, I would cold call a prospect and say, "As you know we mailed out a computer print out about your property… oh, you've never received it? Sorry about that. Tell you what, we'll have a clerk drop it by between six and seven, ok? Great."

I just set my lead for the night, because I was the clerk that was going to come by.

The only time I would fool around with flyers was when I didn't have the prospect's address. When I had a lead with an ethnic name, I had a good feeling that they were potential land buyers. Why? Because in the old country, land was hard to buy. If I did not have their phone number, I could not set up an appointment to pitch them. So I sent them a flyer through the mail – only with a Reverse! Unlike most salespeople who made it a point to spell the prospect's name correctly, I would purposely misspell their name to get a reaction. Prospects would call me up with indignation and pride about the misspelling of their name. This of course is what I wanted — to have them call me. As I ate a little humble pie and apologized for the error, I was now in a position to set up an appointment.

The phone was all I needed in order to get in the door. This type of lead was easy, but other salespeople were critics about my method and said it wasn't a "lead" at all. I would respond by asking them what was a good lead? The best lead I ever heard of was a referral from someone who'd already bought, but any other type of lead — and I don't care how good you think it is — there's no guarantee you will close it.

Cooling the Grief

There was a common problem with most closers in the sales office. When the prospect found out they had been lied to, they would try to get a hold of the salesperson who sold them the deal by calling the office.

Remember Mrs. McMadd from my book *The Sales Trap*? Hy Binder screwed her on a deal and she called the office to get a hold of him. Hy Binder told the receptionist, "Hold all my calls. I'm out of town." Often I heard salespeople blow their calls off by telling the receptionist impatiently, "I'm not here, I'm not here."

I thought it was a waste to have these minimum wage receptionists take the grief calls because they didn't know how to handle them. The only thing the receptionist can do is pacify the prospect by saying, "I'd be glad to tell the salesman when he comes in from out of town that you called." And that's the end of it.

I asked the general manager to let me take those phone calls. He refused, saying that's what they had the receptionist for.

"She's polite. You're a bit rough on the phone," the manager told me.

"But there's gold in that phone," I said. "You're throwing away opportunity!"

I went up to the receptionist and told her to give me the phone anyway.

On the line, the pissed off prospect chewed me out for ten minutes even though I was not the person that sold her the bad deal. When she was finished I said, "I understand how you feel. We've had problems in the past with some of these reps in the office. By the way, how did you hear about that property to begin with? What side of the coast was it one? The right side? Ohhhh! You mean you got a piece of that? I've got an idea how to make this a better deal for you. I'd be willing to come out and talk to you about it between six and seven."

Now I've got her turned around! I let her ventilate by telling her we understand the problem – I'm agreeing with her, to disarm her, and then promote her for another deal (agree, disarm, attack). Well the prospect is happy to have someone come over now, whereas before they would have done anything to keep a pesky salesperson out of their house.

I went over to the prospect's home and heard the whole story of how these sharks pitched her. After she had blown off steam, I offered her an upgrade into a bigger property. I couldn't always pull it off, but when I did it was beneficial for both of us.

The thief that lied to her got a free ride out of trouble because I took care of the prospect's problem. Once they vented, they kept the heat off the office so these lowlifes that did it to them weren't walking around with a price on their heads. I took the grief calls not because I wanted to help get the heat off these bandits, but because I could possibly get a sale or a referral out of it. By upgrading the prospects, they were happy. It was a win-win.

The upgrade would not have happened if I hadn't gotten a hold of the office phone. During my sales career, every manager tried to prevent me from picking up the office phones. They didn't understand how I could make lemonade out of lemons by Reversing a grief call. Had I been able to work *just* the grief calls, I could have turned it into its own cottage industry. The managers were naysayers. You'd think after all the stuff I pulled, they'd never doubt me? They were only shooting themselves in the foot.

These same sales managers were well aware of the fact that many of the closers embellished their presentations to write a deal, and then denied that they were not aware of it. When those grief calls came in, they acted as if they were shocked. Off the record they encouraged that behavior, but on the record they denied it. It was another Reverse.

For the record, if I had grief calls I took care of them myself. It was a Reverse from the conmen who avoided them. They generally didn't want to touch the phone because they were intimidated by it, but I loved it. Before I leave this chapter, I give my best to Alexander Graham Bell.

Naval Gazers in an Ivory Tower

A prospect's attitude is generally guarded. After all, we are talking about his wallet. Whether he's mugged by the local crook or fleeced by a shifty salesperson, his attitude is the same. I rarely met a prospect who said he wasn't burnt. I previously talked about the usual objections. If the salespeople thought they were using mind games against the prospect, the Reverse was he was doing it too. Both are laying traps. Both parties have egos and want to win. The salesperson wants a sale, and the prospect wants to set the conditions if he buys.

Now Reader, remember my attitude: the win-win was preferred, but if there's going to be a loser it's going to be_____. Can you fill in the blank? That's right, it's the prospect.

You must, as I put it, let the prospect suffer a loss but with discretion. For example, using urgency by telling him that the product may or may not be available as an extended offer – you're planting the seed of doubt in his mind that procrastination could cost him an opportunity.

In my opinion, in the long run it is more important that you stay a winner with or without the sale. If the prospect bums you out and messes up your mind with rejection, you have suffered the loss. Salespeople must always win if it's their livelihood. The prospect with a loss can live with it. Remember, this is war.

If I seem to have an attitude that is too rigid for some of you critics, my track record was self evident. I can't tell you how many times some so-called sales expert would tell me how to pitch a deal. I would listen impartially with a smile and of course continue with my same technique.

If some of you salespeople think you're up against hard times with bad leads and an unstable economy, you should have seen what I lived through and how I got around it. I always had naysayers around me, constantly telling me what I couldn't do – which I proceeded to go out and do anyway.

This may be hard to believe but I generally had no training in any of these companies. Sales may be one of the few professions where you need no formal training at all to be successful in the business world. You may be thinking, *How did this guy make a sale without any training?* Remember that salespeople generally go into training every week. There are weekly meetings in almost any sales office. The office does this to make sure their salespeople are still awake, still working, and if they need a shot of adrenaline with a rah-rah meeting to get them pumped up.

I also never had a mentor or a support system from any office. And I certainly was not an expert on the product knowledge of what I sold. If knowledge sold I'd ship a truck of books from the local library onto your lawn. Nothing would get sold. *You sell*. I can tell you that for a fact because I've walked into sales offices without any training and closed a sale that same day.

The best way I can explain my success was my attitude. I'd first sell myself on how to pitch the product or service, and then project it to the prospect. It's another Reverse because I knew that the saying "you have to believe in what you sell" was a crock. I'm not saying I did or did not believe in a product, but I do know that selling is a performance and the prospect is your audience. They applaud you when you close or act like a critic when you don't.

The odd thing was I ended up being the one who trained the trainers. There was a national sales training convention held out of town with sales trainers and company Vice Presidents. My managers told me to say nothing at this meeting. I didn't want to be there to begin with anyway. I knew they were worried because I didn't use their sales manuals which cost them a lot of money. The managers didn't want me saying anything about how I used my own maverick pitch.

Earlier I talked about competition in the office with the inept formal power of some of these managers. Instead of teaching sales techniques that really worked, they usually promoted step-by-step training manuals to the trainees that were so useless I suspect that the prospects were the authors!

So I had to listen to the national sales trainer demonstrate to the attending salespeople how to use their sales manual. When the meeting was over, and I was the last one to leave, the national trainer pulled me aside. He asked me, "How do you use your shotgun pitch? I want to use it."

On the record, I couldn't say anything about it. Off the record, they wanted my pitch. Another Reverse.

Now I'm not going to feign humility; that's hypocritical. I was one of the best in the business. I took credit for my successes as well as my setbacks. I constantly heard from naysayers, "You can't do that." I can't tell you how many times I made believers out of them. My performance spoke for itself. I didn't care one way or the other what the naysayers believed as long as I was rewarded for my ability. They could go back to sucking up coffee and blaming everybody else for their inept sales performance.

There was a time when I left land sales and saw an ad in the paper to sell correspondence courses. I went to the recruiting office and as I went in I saw several people studying training manuals. I asked the sales manager when I could get started.

"You have to go through three days of training," he said.

"I am not going to do that," I told him. "If you want to give me some leads, I'll go out there and bring you back a deal."

The manager was shocked. "That impossible," he said. I shook his hand and left.

As I walked out the door, he ran after me. He stopped me and gave me a handful of leads.

"I'll prove you can't do it. Here's some leads, see what you can do with them." As he hands them over to me with the course catalog, he laughed along with the trainees who were watching me.

That evening I went out, knocked on the first door, and nobody was home. I went to the second door, made a presentation, and didn't close. I went to the third door. All I did was tell the prospect how much I didn't know, and read the course syllabus to them with a negative pitch. Instead of telling the prospect all the reasons why he could qualify, I told him I didn't know if he *could* qualify. In other words, instead of saying, "It's affordable!" I would say "I don't know if you *can* afford it." Again, it's all a performance.

Accepting no excuses, I said to the prospect during the pitch, "Unfortunately, not everyone can qualify for this course. Don't give me twenty reasons why you can't do it, give me one good reason why you can and I'll write it down." This was the close. After they came up with their reason why they should qualify for the course, I said, "Got a pen? Good, make your check out to the correspondence school."

I closed the deal. The next morning I took the deal back to the sales manager and he almost fell over! He not only hired me, he made me the assistant sales manager. To make a long story short, after winning many awards within that company I ended up taking his job.

Audacity

Countless times I used audacity to close a sale. I once made a deal over the phone with a prospect who lived on the other side of the state. He almost *challenged* me to drive over to pitch him at four in the morning. He really didn't think I would do it.

I drove in the middle of the night to catch him before he went out the door. In fact, he had told me that if I could get there *before* he left he would take the deal. I arrived before four in the morning and he was already going out the door anyway! He was trying to sneak out of there just to make sure I didn't get there – but I caught him! I think I wrote him on the deal because I had the audacity to follow through with what I said.

Talk about audacity with attitude, I once called a prospect at two in the morning. He was pissed off, but I still wrote the deal. That wasn't as bad as the Indian doctor that I sold a canal lot to who was criticizing me after the sale. He thought he was really socking it to me when he said, "You know, you are not a very good salesman. You make the sale but you put too much pressure on people."

I casually responded, "Aw geez doc, I didn't realize. Y'know, I'm still learning. I'll try to improve myself."

All day long I would be thrilled to receive these criticisms…*after* I wrote the sale, that is.

As previously stated, creative salespeople are independent contractors who at times float from deal to deal. After starting at another company, I entered the office to find it full of old desks with dust all over them. As with any sales organization I worked for, all I required from them was a desk, a phone, and a private cubbyhole. I picked out one of the dusty desks, and happened to open the drawer to find it loaded with old leads.

I asked the manager, "Can I have these?"

He said, "Yeah, we were going to throw them out anyway."

With audacity I said, "I'll tell you what, I'll write the first one off the top."

He looked at me and rolled his eyes with whole office chuckling behind him. The way I looked at it, if I didn't write it, what did I lose? *But what if I did*? Either way, I had said it for effect.

Of course I went out that night and didn't end up writing the first one off the top – I wrote two! Now the office manager thought I walked on water. However, invariably one of the parasitic salesmen came out from under the rocks saying, "That was my lead from seven years ago! You owe me on that lead!" Yet again some salesperson found a way to get into my pocket and I had to give him a piece of my action.

I was one of the top producers in the company on my way to winning the National Sales Contest. Although I was working in land sales, I felt I could sell housing just as well but I wasn't in the housing division. To get into sales for the housing division was a month's orientation on how to make the three hour sales pitch in somebody's home.

Out of curiosity one day, while making a lot sale the prospect mentioned that he was thinking of buying a condo from the company. As soon as he said that, I started to pitch him a condo deal. I had no training whatsoever. I couldn't even *legally* write the housing contract because I was in the land sales division, but I wrote it anyway.

I took it back to the office to show the general manager. He was awed.

"What am I going to do with this?" he said.

"I don't care what you do with it. I wrote it."

He called in the general sales manager from the housing division. When he came my manager presented the contract to him and said, "Ken just wrote a condo contract."

"He couldn't have done that!" the housing manager was shocked.

"Here it is. He did it."

"That's not possible!" the housing division manager said. "That's a month's training!"

"Well there it is. What do we do with it?" my manager asked.

"I don't know what to do with it! How could he have done it without any training?"

They argued back and forth until I grabbed the contract back and said, "I don't care what you want to do with it. I'll tear it up if you don't want it."

"Oh no, no, no!" they both protested. It was a problem for them, but they were just greedy enough to allow it.

To my knowledge, I became the only sales rep in that company that could work out of two divisions. As it turned out, the Reverse was that the housing manager who was a naysayer later on told me he went up and down the East Coast of America and "couldn't find another Ken George." He was probably my strongest supporter after that, as I went on to win the housing division's national sales title as top producer.

There was another time when another sales manager doubted my ability to write a sale. Working out of the land sales division, a mail-in lead came in that nobody wanted because the prospect was out of state. The office manager handed it to me after the other salespeople had passed on it.

"Here's a lead for you Ken," he told me like he was doing me a big favor. "If you can write this lead, I'll buy you dinner."

I said, "I guess I'll have to call long distance, then."

"Do it on your own dime," my sales manager told me. "The office won't pick up the tab if you run up the phone bill."

I made the call out of my own pocket. After about twenty minutes of pitching the prospect, he said, "I want to tell you something. You'll never believe who's sitting next to me right now."

"Who?" I asked.

"One of your competitors from a local office is here, sitting right next to me. He's been trying to pitch me for months. You've told me more in a few minutes than he's told me in all that time! Send the contract in and I'll sign it."

I immediately went up to my manager and told him I had made the deal. He pointed to his palm and said, "When hair grows on my hand will that deal come in the mail!" He didn't believe me.

The contract didn't come in right away because of the time it takes to send mail through the post office. A week later, it came in. My manager was floored. The other salespeople in the office couldn't believe it.

I called the prospect back to confirm that I'd received his contract. He said, "By the way, I'd like to buy a condominium while you're at it." So I sold him a condominium, too. It once again awed everyone. The office hadn't even wanted to pick up the tab on the phone call, and here I had written two sales out of a lead nobody wanted.

The same sales manager who had given me the lead told me, "You're the greatest salesman I ever met." He choked on it, but he said it all the same. The out-of-state deal was another case of them handing me a garbage lead, and acting like they'd given me a gift. And I Reversed them.

Morality

To some of you holier-than-thou critics who think that some of my techniques were marginal, I would like to remind you that this is not heaven on earth. We live in a competitive market economy where survival of the fittest is the name of the game. My techniques justify to me what it takes to be a winner in a modern society. Winning cannot just be about sales because salespeople hear the word *"no"* so many times more than they hear the word yes. If you don't maintain your dignity, all these rejections will overwhelm you.

If you critics think I could get away with my Reverse techniques because I didn't have the same financial obligations as other salespeople, think again! I had a family to provide for with no safety nets, and no support from anybody. I was seldom intimidated by the prospects because my lifestyle was generally under control. I was usually prepared with a plan B for a rainy day. I didn't blow my commissions as so many salespeople did. What's your excuse? Control does not start at the pitch remember – control is how you live your life.

Perhaps I didn't act like an altar boy all the time, but I was no worse than any other businessman. Again, I didn't say I was wearing any halos. Certainly I was a moral step above what the sharks in the business were actually doing. Now I've acknowledged that I'm no saint, so let's get over that one. And if you critics want to pursue it, remember people who live in glass houses and etcetera, so let's not go down that road.

And by the way, I've got a truth question for you critics: if the shoe was on the other foot, what would you have done? What about that implied halo you're wearing? Yeah, that's what I thought – see you on Sunday in the front pew.

The Reverse is that those who seem to do nothing are the first to criticize those who do something. I wonder if they're fractured egos are showing? As a creative salesperson, I was motivated within and I didn't give a rat's @$$ about what critics think.

Many times there were naysayers who attacked me with the moral question, "Did you lie?! Salespeople are thieves."

I Reversed them by saying, "Let me ask you something, what do you do for a living? You're an engineer? So building tanks that blow up people is okay? Oh, I see."

A woman at one of my seminars told me, "You know, you're being a bit deceptive."

I said, "I will admit at times I fudged, but what do you do for a living?"

She said, "I work down at the drugstore."

"Oh I see, you sell cigarettes that can lead to cancer. Do you really want to go down that road?"

After I addressed the argument, I continued with what I was saying. Did you catch that, salespeople? *Answer the objection and then get off the subject.*

At times I might agree with the critic by saying, "Yes, I'm guilty. However, don't let the perfect be the enemy of the good. It's not okay for me to blue sky? I see. But it's okay for some merchants to trade only in cash so they don't have to report even their tips on their taxes? Or sell overpriced products and services? Shall I go on? We all rationalize our deeds, especially those of you who sit in the front pew of your place of worship. I'm no angel, I already told you that."

There seems to be no shortage of sideline wimpy critics who add very little to any positive results. To get off with trying to justify their mutterings, they call it "constructive criticism." Doesn't that sound familiar Reader? My response to them is, "Get some talent first, then you can run your mouth." What they may be criticizing is creative sales, such as the Reverse. My technique is just that. If my memory serves me, many of these critics were ex-salespeople that couldn't cut it in the arena to begin with.

Many fast-track sales types that could close as well as I could were even on record saying that at times if they could choose between a lie and the truth, they're more comfortable with the lie.

My motives for why I pitched with the truth was not just because of morality, but because it was a Reverse. No one was prepared for the truth. If I'm telling it straight, I don't have to mentally trip over new lies to cover up the last lie.

Yes, there are moments during a pitch that I embellished, but it didn't affect the outcome of the sale one way or another

– no more than most promoters in business anywhere. From car salesman to rug peddlers to the aluminum siding guys, they will spin a tale. If they're not spinning you openly, they're doing it by omission. Chances are, if I fell into a guilty category at times, it was by omission.

The only difference between me and other salespeople who blue-skied was I was usually better at it, but I never hurt anybody. I would never tell a flat lie. I had a lot of pride in myself. I knew that anybody could lie, but to sell a product or service straight was real class. I pitched the prospect in increments, conditioning their mind to accept my strategy slowly but surely, commitment by commitment. So in the end I told them the whole truth, locking them into the deal with their own words.

Most of these salespeople that were questioning their own abilities would question mine as well. Personally I think they were too insecure and professionally jealous that someone could do what they couldn't.

There were even sales types who talked behind my back, saying I was getting secret deals on the side. Every time, as it turned out, it was again just professional jealousy with no foundation for what they said. Even when they confronted me saying, "We know you're playing games," I asked them where was the evidence? What did they think they had on me? That question usually shut them up as they went back to their coffee machine.

It was insinuation. If enough people are spreading rumors, it turned a molehill into a mountain when really there's nothing. When they took me on, one-by-one they usually apologized and came to have respect for me afterwards. If they liked me as well, that was secondary. Some did and others didn't.

It's amazing how many critics will read this book and have their opinions on what I did. They'll probably offer their unsolicited moral assessments of all salespeople by saying, "I wouldn't do what you did." Closer to the truth may be that they were not *capable* of doing it.

My answer to that is to look in the mirror sometime at their own profession. Look at the many ways they've scammed their own employer chewing up the clock talking about baseball scores and not finishing their projects on straight time, which rewards them so they can come in on double-time. But that's alright? They're hiding behind a major corporation claiming it's a part of "doing business as usual."

What these prospects forget is that if salespeople do not sell their company's products and services, their own 9-to-5 jobs would be worthless. They don't realize that the "lowly salesperson" is their benefactor. Now isn't that a Reverse? I'm referring to the sales rep drop-outs who ran back to the safety of a 9-to-5 job of alleged security and a paycheck. For the record, before anyone takes offense, I have nothing for or against 9-to-5 jobs, corporate jobs, the unions, or any other support group. I am saying that anyone who is critical of salespeople is generally not in favor of the opportunity that some of us welcome – a chance to be our own rugged individualist in a profession where the sky is the limit based on our abilities.

So Mr. Critic, get over your two-bit opinion and accept your fate: some of you are just quitters. If you had any character, you could have made it in creative sales even without talent. Simply work the numbers. With all the *no*'s you hear, eventually someone is going to say *yes*. But you could not have gotten to the yes if you were not willing to do the due diligence called *work* by knocking on doors that an immigrant off the boat does successfully. Naysayers have criticized his success as well. So enough with the criticism and hiding behind the safety of your desk. You almost give salespeople a worse stereotype than even the suede shoe artists.

The Stuff of Dreams

I'd see these motivational speakers come into these offices years ago and I would think, *They're paying them... to do that?* I felt I knew more than they did! At the beginning of my sales career, when I was still very naïve, I thought everybody knew more than I did. I just wanted to keep up with them. I wanted to be *as good as them*, never "the best." Then old Sweet Willy screwed me in that contest, and he woke me out of my lethargy.

I still think about what he did for me. In his head he must have wished to God he never did that because he had to compete with me forever after that. It wasn't exactly the heist of the century, but it was an epiphany for me. The subtle realization that I could be the best... thank you, Willy! You unconsciously helped me to shape my sales career as it stands today.

When something is stolen from me, I'm motivated even more. I don't take it as a loss, just a setback. When a prospect cancelled a deal on me, it was like a kick in the stomach. In about fifteen minutes I would get over it, and I'm on to the next prospect with a vengeance. I want to get it back. It's another Reverse. Just like when the other salespeople found a way to mooch from my deals, I had the choice to quit or be creative. I chose to get creative.

For a salesperson, your worst nightmare is a cancellation. After a prospect cancelled one of my deals, I was motivated to get it back *in spades*. I already told you the story of how Willy pirated a sale from my friend and claimed I would get the credit for it. For revenge I didn't just take one deal away from Willy, I took several.

Contrary to what most salespeople are motivated by, I was motivated more by winning than by money. In other words, I would have preferred to make less money as number one than more money in second place. There's a difference between being in first place and being number one.

Winning is a state of mind. You don't worry about any individual sale whether you make it or you don't. If you don't sell this guy, you go after the next one. With that kind of confidence you're in control and you'll probably close several deals. But as I said, you never want to give the impression to the prospect that you live or die by what he does or doesn't do.

After winning these contests, it was a downer for me as if my balloon had been deflated. After I went through all that work, in the next moment it's done. I'd think, *Now I have to start over again.* Now that's something most salespeople never talk about. Most depression for salespeople comes from simply hearing the word *no*. I'm sharing a Reverse here, that even after winning the contest I felt depressed because I had won something that took so long to achieve and it was all over in a fleeting moment.

I have heard of many salespeople feeling good after they achieved their goals. It was a Reverse for me; it was more about the process and not just the goal. Most people begrudgingly work towards a goal or reward. On the contrary, I loved what I did. It was never about the money or awards, but I knew I was going to get them anyway. So when I finally achieved my results, I thought, *I went through all this and there's no more?* Like that song by Peggy Lee when the little girl's house burns down I thought, *Is that all there is?*

Winning for me was like the stuff of dreams. I wanted to be among the best. I was unaffected by outside motivation because I thought it could weaken me. I was always *motivated within* and impervious to naysayers who said I "couldn't do it." I was able to not focus on the goal, but the results instead. In my opinion, goals are all talk; a rationalization salespeople sometimes use to satisfy their guilt for the moment when they aren't making any progress. I had to see the result in my mind in order to complete my goals. I suspect anybody who talks about their goals – with little actually getting done – gets so hyped up that in their mind they already think they've done it. They seldom end up completing the task.

To just talk about something is to act like it's done when it's not, and you're just psyching yourself up for a short while. In my experience, I never saw people who talked about their goals over and over again, and actually accomplish them. The salesperson who doesn't talk about it and just plows ahead, generally achieves their results. There are talkers and then there are doers.

At one of my earlier employments at a sales organization, another salesman who started out with me went out right away and bought himself a new car. I asked him why he didn't wait to have the new car as his goal.

He said, "Oh, no. The fact that I *bought* the car will drive me to do well in sales."

I thought that was so flaky! A few weeks later he quit, but he still had those car payments coming in.

I always thought in Reverse from that type of mentality – I would have rationalized that *if* I achieved the results, I *might* buy a car. I'd never go out and buy it first.

Master Plan

Creative sales is not just about making sales. It's about how much rejection you can handle to get to the sale. To make a sale is wonderful – it's like winning a game. It's not how good you can win, it's how bad you can lose – that's a Reverse! How do you cope with a sale that cancels? If you don't have a stomach for rejection, generally you won't make it in sales.

Listen to these stats: if you think small business has a bad batting average of around 90% closing shop and quitting within the first year, in sales it might be 2% that survive. Of those closers who are survivors, many of them are scam artists. As I pointed out, I was no angel because I blue-skied, but I did it with integrity. To me a lie was such an embarrassment with no class – I wouldn't let myself sink so low as to consider the notion that I would have to lie in order to close a sale.

Whenever I was alone to think, ideas would usually come into my head. Many times these ideas worked in creating something from nothing, and other times they didn't. I had a dozen *great* ideas when I was working in these companies; like coming up with a master plan to promote the canal lots, the ad book, and even using the yellow pages. Usually I found creative simple ways to survive in the field of sales. I certainly wasn't counting on others to do it for me.

To me motivation is an adrenaline rush. Money was not the issue. I know for the sharks it was always a problem with some creditor chasing them. That was never the case was me. If you were after the money, you've already lost control because you probably didn't prepare for a rainy day. My goal was to win; the money never had any control over me, as I lived a conservative lifestyle which was not dependent on how much I made.

Generally when I conceived of a concept, I instantly knew how to implement it. The first person to be sold was not the prospect, it was me. That's a Reverse. If I was sold, I was confident that I could sell it to the prospect. That does not mean that I believed in the product or service, one way or the other. The fact is I've sold products that I did not necessarily believe in. Of all the psycho babble that is out there, it is certainly convenient for salespeople who do believe it… but I was sold *on the idea* that it could be sold to the prospect either way.

All of you sociology critics relax with that politically correct stuff you pitched to the students. I am talking about the real world instead of theory or what you read out of a book. A salesperson can use their imagination to come up with a master plan they can implement to fruition with the brain that God gave us. Take your chance, right or wrong.

Sometimes I suspect that these same professors are threatened by sales types who are successful without the excessive training and tuition fees that feed their tenor. And when many of their graduates are thrown into the real world, they don't seem to have a clue on how to survive. I suspect some of you academic types might suffer the same reality if you were out of your ivory tower and in the streets.

I never relied on some else's ideas – as I said, I was always *motivated within*. Even if the scam artists I alluded to could give me some kind of support, I didn't want it. I counted on myself, which was a wise decision. In other words, when you strip away options, salespeople are forced to either quit or become creative. Being motivated within like this was a trait I learned as a kid with a paper route.

The problem is many salespeople have been controlled by others who do their thinking for them. They move like lemmings in a crowd, and any creative juices they have dry up along with the control of their lives. So how are they supposed to control the prospects?

Streets Paved with Gold

Now many salespeople think that to be in sales you have to be a talented closer. That helps, but I would much rather have an immigrant off the boat than a talented closer on my team. Why? Because when I told a closer he could make six figures by just knocking on doors, he would say to me, "How many doors DO I HAVE TO knock on?"

The immigrant would say "How many doors CAN I knock on."

Do you notice the difference? The immigrant saw opportunity – which is all he wanted – whereas the American worker wants guarantees.

As a kid in the early 40s, where I grew up most families were broke as we were. I remember trying to satisfy one of my biological urges of life – getting lunch. In order to pay for it (when I wasn't taking it out of little girl's desks) I would hustle empty coke bottles in the field for the two cents deposit. I didn't have to do it that often because when I was old enough to have a paper route, I felt like the richest kid on the block. After that I never had to ask anybody for money or hustle coke bottles for lunch again.

I was inner motivated. With a paper route, there was always a sales promotion for an award, like trips around the country just for getting new customers to buy newspapers. For me it was like shooting fish in a barrel! I couldn't figure out why other guys weren't doing the same thing. Weren't they motivated enough to win free awards? From what I saw, they preferred their booze and cigarettes in the garage while wasting time talking about sports.

In those days however, there were also other guys who did take every advantage to hustle for a buck. Today it seems that many people are looking for guarantees and when they're taken away they seem to fall on their face, complaining and blaming everyone else for their dilemma. Then I look at the immigrant who comes over to America with a language barrier, a different cultural upbringing, and the only thing he wants is *opportunity,* not *guarantees.* The immigrant sees the streets paved with gold. They often work long hours with no support from anyone else, and end up owning most of the businesses in the area. I constantly hear the American born criticize them instead of learning from them.

How often have I heard people using the immigrant as a scapegoat, claiming they're "taking our jobs?" The truth is they create their own jobs, working long hours at gas stations and party stores. Very few of them had any capital to begin with. They're risk takers who saved their own money and became their own bosses.

I saw the same situation in creative sales when the immigrants came in. They were rarely closers, but with a language and culture barrier to overcome, they simply worked the numbers. They made phone calls and knocked on doors. I rarely heard them complaining, even though they had the same ups and downs as other salespeople.

I've heard critics say there are no more opportunities in this country. I'll say again, there are always opportunities in sales, especially creative sales. So please don't cop out with that old bromide that sales is not for everybody. Again, sales is basically just numbers – if you're willing to work them and handle rejection. Sales is something when there is nothing else. And for the record, how would you know if you never tried it?

The immigrants are the new generation of entrepreneurs. To them the glass is not half empty, but half full. They know how to create something from nothing. They are practicing the same program our grandfathers did in the 1950s. They're willing to pay the price by trying to build up their own business. Instead of criticizing them, we should be emulating them.

In these tough economic times, who do you think is the last guy standing?

When jobs are being lost, there is always sales. Living in an affluent society, we tend to take for granted what we have that most of the rest of the world doesn't have: opportunity. However, to survive one has to deal with rejection and setbacks. The body count of failures opposed to survivors who make it in the sales game is lopsided. The Reverse is the immigrant similar to the creative salesperson who did not have the advantages, will generally make it.

Now this is not necessarily a criticism of the American born, but it's generally a fact of this modern society. And comparing both in the end, who do you think has the advantage? Is it possibly the last guy standing, or is it a consequence of our culture?

The oxymoron is that it is only human to build a society with all the advantages. Unfortunately we seem to have so many people that were not prepared for a rainy day. Maybe we should consider adjusting our attitude and learn like the immigrant to be prepared so that when we have a setback, we are prepared for it with a plan B.

When an immigrant criticizes the work ethic of this country, critics say he's being anti-American but that's not true. He's telling the truth, so it's easy for others to use them as a scapegoat. It's just like people who don't go to church and say, "I'm not one of those hypocrites who sits in the front pew. God knows I'm a good person." It's a lot of crap – that person is just too lazy to go to church. So he uses the guy *in* the church (whom he's possibly right about) as an excuse to scapegoat him to get him off the hook of going to church himself. They're both bad, it's just a matter of degree.

Here's the truth: many Americans spend a fortune in academia to hopefully get the big job, which is okay until you lose it. Now what do you do for an encore? The Reverse is the salesperson who may or may not be formally educated, like the immigrant, is never out of work until his last sale, then he immediately goes back to work selling. Interesting, eh? What do you think Reader?

Academia

There's no mystery to set up most any business if you are a risk taker. How to create a business in the real world is different from what is generally taught in school, in college, or in the unions. Thinkers just think, while doers get it done. And if they make a mistake, they correct it and move on. But if you're just thinking you'll never launch. Again, paralysis by analysis.

If these "brightest and best" of the current graduating class do decide to start a business, they may take out a business loan. But if they can't think outside of the box and blow that start-up money, what do they do for an encore? They're out of business and still have a debt to pay back!

However, the immigrant coming off the boat, no matter what happens will survive even without a business loan because he can think outside the box with street smarts. With all the faults we have here, America is still the best place to be for business and opportunity. So what is anybody's excuse for not pursuing it?

Some professors in academia tell their students, "You've got to get your Master's Degree to make it in the business world."

What are they doing for these students? They're taking the students' money for the class, which gives the professor a guaranteed paycheck. Now the student has to go out and implement their so-called theories.

I'll tell you this, if some of the professors didn't have that plantation mentality of tenor in academia, and they were out in the real world to compete with the average immigrant, they couldn't make it! The immigrant is motivated by the opportunity in this country. Can academia say as much for the average student who is getting educated to go into the business world?

Teachers may want to modify their lesson plans to the tried and true prove techniques of successful creative salespeople if they really want to help the student. Many teachers are comfortable in academia because they can play it safe there. They can rattle off all their theories and shove it down the throats of the students who are at the mercy of the grade the professors will give them. They can play dictator to the students who pay an arm and a leg to some of these ego-centric scholars, and are paid whether the students fails or passes. Not a bad deal for them.

I'm not out to offend the quality teachers who are out there. I've found that generally the smartest guys who make the best teachers are the ones with practical knowledge who are really out in the trenches during the day and come in to teach at night. They know because they're out doing it, and that's a teacher that deserves respect. At the same time, there are a lot of them who are so burned out after the job that they don't have the energy or the time to teach a class how to make it out there in the real world.

Students that I've spoken to have been excited about my definition of a successful creative salesperson. The general reaction is, "Wow! Where'd this come from? I never heard it before in academia."

I've talked to students as well as adults, and when they hear these concepts from me they've often commented that they wished they'd known them earlier.

Personally, I wish someone had taught *me* this stuff when I was a kid. I would have skipped over the years

I spent at a corporation. I was a misfit there because my imagination was wasted in a 9-to-5 atmosphere where you have to play ball in order to survive the political structure of the office, all the while being paid flunky money. In the real world of creative sales, you're out in the trenches. If you sell something that's a big ticket item you're paid for it because of your ability and the sky is the limit.

Our society does not seem to teach enough students survival skills. Creative sales possibly can. I'm not advocating that all students make sales a career, but it possibly could be the most fortunate training they could receive to cope with everyday life.

They would learn at least to take responsibility for their performance – or lack of it. They will soon discover that it does not matter if you pour out your heart and soul with a near-miss of closing a sale. It doesn't count for anything when you're going to the bank. This isn't horseshoes.

They will learn to deal with reality – that you must be successful. If not, the wolves are still at the door waiting for their money. Students will finally get it. No amount of whining will matter. They'll realize that unless they score a sale, they can't pay the bills. In sales they won't get a free ride provided by Uncle Sam with a safety net. Now that's a Reverse.

Opportunity Now

I was approached by a dermatologist once who hyped me up on the idea of selling a special line of his cosmetics. Once I dedicated my time to marketing the material, he walked away leaving me with all the responsibility and no financial backing. I learned that I needed to get a commitment from the other party first, before making a move myself in any future ventures.

Years later during a period of recession and massive factory layoffs, a retired PhD asked me to get involved with a proposed consulting business. It was something I had been considering in the past so I agreed... under the condition that the PhD started a few of the accounts first.

In three months time he came back telling me he couldn't get the venture off the ground. He said that it was too hard to start a business, let alone one that involved consulting for sales and human resources.

"Watch this," I said after listening to him. "I'll show you how to do it on my lunch hour."

I took a newspaper filled with sales ads – the only types of jobs hiring at the time of the layoffs – and called one of them. Once I had the sales ad manager on the phone, I said to him, "I see you're recruiting for salespeople. Can I ask you, what did you pay for this ad?"

When he told me I said, "What if I could – for half the price you paid for this ad – put you in front of a captive audience where you can make your presentation to recruit for ten minutes?"

The manager was excited at this idea. Not only did it cut his budget in half, but he was being guaranteed an audience. After a dozen phone calls of the same nature, I had nine managers from different sales organizations lined up to make presentations.

I then called various radio and TV stations, telling them I had a public service bulletin to help people get jobs. They were more than happy to invite me on their shows to make my pitch. Next, I called the local mayors of various towns who were equally excited about the idea. Several of them offered to lend their civic center auditoriums to me. These auditoriums were used for the sales organizations to pitch the unemployed workforce that had heard about the event from their local radio and television programs.

Still on my lunch break, I went down to city hall and registered for my DBA (doing business as) *Opportunity Now*. The DBA cost about $10 out of pocket, and didn't cost anybody else *anything* to put together the program. The only cash flow going in or out was the organizations payment to me for half of the advertisement fee. Next I opened up a PO Box over the border for the consulting business, and *Opportunity Now* instantly became an international organization.

All of this was created with a few phone calls and a $10 bill; practically nothing. Thus, I was able to once again *create something from nothing*.

So, what came out of the presentations *Opportunity Now* put on? The program to bring laid off workers into the sales business was a hit. A local insurance company built their entire sales force from the program. Even though most people can't survive in the business of sales, it kept up some laid off workers' motivation and momentum while they were out of work. Some stayed in the field of sales, but most were called back to their factory jobs. I simply created a business that excelled at bringing the unemployed and the companies seeking workers together.

A representative of the employment security commission became involved after the initial sales presentation, and thought that *Opportunity Now* was too good to be true, and thus a scam. They called me out on public radio, saying I was a fraud. A local radio station invited me to debate the allegation over the live airwaves. I accepted. Five minutes into the debate, the representative of the commission apologized, retracted his charge, and even asked me to do promotions and consulting *work for him*. That's a Reverse.

Bear in mind I was still running number one in competitive land sales during this time. I was able to start my own business while still performing at the top. I didn't need a loan or outside financing for a start-up company. I required virtually no planning or aid from any "mentors." I just sat down and created it during my lunch hour what the PhD couldn't figure out in three months time.

Character and Characters

My pal Sweet Willy wasn't exactly a "paradigm of virtue" (to quote Willy himself). He had great talent for being the top producer in that company for years, but he didn't trust himself. He was never sold on his own credibility and that was his Achilles Heel. When salespeople like him ducked away from the phones or told people, "Can I help you?" they couldn't swallow their own crap. And they knew that's exactly what it was. If I was helping somebody, I didn't say it, I just did it.

I really get a kick out of the time he told me, "You know Ken, I have to admit… you're *slightly* more honest than I am."

I generally acted like I didn't hear what somebody else told me – especially Willy – but I had to really keep my poker face that time to keep from cracking up. Even when my peers were praising me I wouldn't show them any emotion. There were times in my career when I didn't have any idea how to generate my next sale. I'd start to doubt my own abilities at times like that. But I never told anybody. It seemed to bother some salespeople I appeared so controlled.

Willy had contacts – he knew bankers, doctors, lawyers, and other high-end professionals. He was well known for writing big ticket deals while I wrote in mass volume with bread-and-butter deals. I never had the big contacts. I had to write several accounts to catch up to one of his.

I was in my office one day when he and my manager approached me and asked me to write my deals in Willy's name so he could win the national sales contest. I was furious at the fact that they'd even ask me that. When my manager put the pressure on me, I reluctantly agreed. I fell on my own sword at that moment because by agreeing to help Willy, I was writing myself out of the competition.

Willy came up and put his arm around me with a smile, and said, "Of course, next year I'll write my deals in your name, Ken."

"I don't need your help, Willy," I said. "I can win without you."

I let Willy and the manager know I had some class and would never ask for their help. It wasn't because I had false pride. If I had accepted his offer for help, it would weaken me to depend on somebody for help in the future. Further, there was no way Sweet Willy was going to keep his end of the bargain anyway. I wasn't going to get anything out of him even if I said yes. I knew all of that up front, so I never took his "help" or anyone else's.

The next year, I won the national sales contest all on my own.

Now I don't want to give the impression that Willy was just another slippery suede shoe salesman. He could be charming as well. It was a love-hate relationship because we were competitors. He was a step above the parasite fleecing managers who lived off of my overrides. Willy had class, and I respected his abilities.

As for the managers, there were a couple of them I respected for their ability as well. Not *all* of them were political appointments who didn't have talent. Too many of them, however, were into my pocket with skim-scam rules they were coming up with that allowed them to take a piece of my action on top of my overrides.

I didn't respect the ones who didn't have the ability to do it themselves.

So why did I stay in the sales business when I felt so many people were screwing me? Not only because land sales was a big ticket item, but because I *enjoyed* it. It never felt like work to me. If I could do it all over again, I would. I was the idea guy who could create something from nothing.

There were a lot of closers just as good as me, but many of them were not shy about bending the truth, saying or doing anything to get the deal. Now my boy Willy could do it with polish; that was the only difference. His ego wouldn't let him be just another conman. He thought he was a step above.

At times there were a couple of these hustlers who would come up and ask me how I made so many deals. They couldn't figure it out with the way I dressed and my low profile. One guy said to me, "You dress like a loser, but why the put on? You can't be *that* lucky all the time with those deals you're bringing in."

Many times when the slam dunk artists scored a sale, they'd beat the drum and brag about it. It was such a turn off. Willy however would do it in a classy way by strutting around with his contracts. "Had a bad night," he'd say, "I only wrote four." The other salesmen would be salivating at their desks, knowing they hadn't scored that many in a *month*.

They would have a good time at the expense of the prospects who put money in their pocket with a deal. I wrote about this in satire in my book *The Sales Trap* – you can read the first chapter of it as a bonus add-on at the back of this book. When I saw these scam artists celebrating after they "took a sucker down" and laughing, it was annoying because it stereotyped the rest of us. I personally resented that attitude because I was grateful to any prospect that I was able to write so that I could provide for my family. To many other salespeople, a prospect was just another sucker they conned into a deal.

The truth was, back in those days of the land sales, nobody realized how valuable that property really was that we sold. They were connivers who moved on to other deals. The Reverse was that the properties double and tripled in value when they were developed. I should have been buying it, as well as selling it! Personally I did buy one, and its value went up a great deal by the time I resold it to a grateful buyer. Later when I was a broker, I bought back many of these same properties that I had sold. It was a win-win. Buyers made a profit on their purchase, and I also made a profit by flipping them again.

When these hit-and-run artists left the land sales game, they thought it was over. Reader, if you are still awake, I don't want to get ahead of myself in this illuminating story. So suck up some coffee to keep your eyes open. I am well aware that as I write this book, that real estate values have again been devalued. With that said, please allow me to continue.

Because I had a different attitude about sales, these characters were often a hindrance to me. There was a time my manager allocated several lots to me to sell over the weekend. I went out and sold them. In the meantime, my manager got lucky that weekend and sold all of his allocation. He needed more inventory, so he arbitrarily sold all of mine without asking me! When I returned to the office on Monday morning and found out, he shrugged me off.

"Hey kid, you're just going to have to sell some other lots," he said.

Yeah, *rots of ruck!* Think about that – how are you supposed to fight with your manager who's competing directly against you? That was one month's worth of income that he took from me, and now he wanted me to go back to the prospects and try to re-sell them on a different property! Of all the things in sales, that is the most difficult to do. Telling a prospect you just sold the same lot to another buyer and now you want to sell them a different one makes you lose your credibility with them, and thus lose the sale.

It's bad enough that I had to compete in the office with my peers and managers, and then go out and pitch the prospects. On top of all that I was also had to proofread my own contracts typed up by the secretaries who screwed up. Whenever they made a typing error, they were in a position to kill a deal.

Just as important as writing the deal itself, I had to cover my butt to make sure that the contract was typed correct. I never wanted to go back to a customer I just closed and try to explain to them that there's been a mistake on the pricing, especially if the price is *more*.

I learned this lesson the hard way. I set up a joint venture and had the prospects sign the contract. I took it to the office for the secretary to type up. Not paying attention to what she was doing, she put the rate in Canadian dollars instead of American dollars. The prospects took one look at the contract and walked out the door. The mistyped contract blew my credibility with the prospects because they thought I had lied about the price. I never got them back.

I went back to the secretary who had typed it up and said, "You've made a mistake, here."

She looked up at me indifferent, saying, "Well everybody makes mistakes."

I was exasperated. "Do you realize that this deal was possibly equal to your *annual income*? And now it's gone because you didn't proofread? It's simple – you read the price and then type it."

That was a tough setback, considering my own office killed the deal.

<u>*Three Strikes You're Out "Oh what a tangled web we weave, when first we practice* to *deceive."*</u>

In the past I had an associate who was somewhat of a hot shot. He was a good looking guy who resembled Cary Grant, but nobody could trust him. If you saw him and saw me you'd pick him first until you realized he was superficial and I was substance (as he himself said to me once).

On one occasion I gave him a chance to buy lots from an owner for me at an almost give-away price. I said I would give him 20% from the profits when I resold them, but I said he had to come up with some cash first. I wanted to make sure he put in his own personal commitment into the transaction. He agreed, but never came up with the money. When you're given an opportunity to turn a small down payment into a hefty profit you beg and borrow to come up with the cash, but he couldn't do it. He lost his first opportunity with me.

Again I gave my associate another chance to make some money by giving him several leads to go out and pitch. When he was pitching the prospects he liked to impress them by dropping names, which generally turned them off. He did not write any of the leads, and came back into the office saying nobody was interested.

In front of the whole office, I took his leads and pinned one of them up on the wall saying, "I want to thank you in advance for this contribution you've given to my family."

"What contribution?" he said. "Those leads are garbage."

"I intend to write this lead," I told him.

I went out, worked those leads, and wrote half of them. One of them happened to be a huge commission. I went back to the office and in front of everyone I thanked my associate for his "generous gift." I never heard the term "garbage leads" in that office again. And so my associate lost his second opportunity with me.

The best yet was when this same associate did an end run on me. I told him he was to keep his mouth shut about my strategies on selling lots. No sooner did he agree that he went out on the side and pitched some investor into buying several recreational lots. He told the investor that he would then re-sell the lots at a big profit and they would financially both do very well.

He never sold the first lot – he just wasn't a closer, even though he knew my techniques. I had told him all about pitching, but like a good comedian's joke it's all about the timing. He couldn't pull it off, and the investor was stuck with lots that were costing him substantial money in back taxes.

My associate never bothered to tell me that he went behind my back. Instead, he skipped town when the heat was on from the investor. By a fluke I called up the same investor about selling property. He mentioned my associate by name and asked if I was friends with him.

"I know him," I said.

"If you're like him, I don't want to talk to you!" he said. "He's got money out of my pocket and now he's skipped town!" He told me what had happened and I immediately saw an opportunity to create something from nothing.

"Maybe I can be your benefactor," I told him. "I can relieve you of those lots."

I offered to buy the lots off of him at a fraction of what he had paid. He wasn't too happy with that offer, but suggested we meet in person at his office. When I declined, he compromised and we met at his attorney's office.

When I arrived, I asked him for the maps of the lots.

"I hold the maps," he said. "Give me a deposit for them."

"What did you say?" I said, somewhat surprised.

"I want a deposit."

"I'm not giving you five cents," I said. "Hand over the maps or there's no deal."

"What the matter?" he smirked. "You can't afford it?"

That remark was enough for me. I walked right out of the office.

I thought that was the end of it until the next day the investor's wife called me up saying, "My husband can be a real @$$." I told her I had found that out first hand. She suggested we renegotiate.

"Look," I told her, "he's not getting a nickel out of me and I'm taking the maps before I go any further."

When I went back to the attorney's office, this time the investor reluctantly bit his tongue and handed over the maps. We agreed on a deal.

Eventually I sold all the lots on land contracts. I accomplished the mission that my associate allegedly told the investor he would do. I spun off all of the property and made a neat profit. After they were sold, the investor who had been conned by my associate apologized to me.

"I didn't know what type of guy you were," he said. "Since you knew that associate of yours, I figured birds of a feather...."

I told him, "You don't know me. You prejudged me. I do exactly what I say I'm going to do."

He was impressed and told me, "I wish I would have gone into business with someone like you." A Reverse! That was a nice concession from him when he realized I honored my commitments.

Eventually my associate crawled out from under the rock he had been hiding under. I went up to him and said, "By the way, I want to thank you."

"For what?" he asked.

"I want to thank you for the deals you put in my lap with your last scam."

"What deals?"

"The ones you didn't bother to tell me about when you tried to pull an end run on me. You broke your commitment to me about never using my strategy. I went and bought those lots from the investor and resold them for a huge commission."

Talk about poetic justice! Actually, by me stepping up and buying the property from the investor he conned, I was also doing my associate a favor by taking the heat off of him.

And so my associate lost his third and final opportunity to make any money with me. He tried to rip me off by doing an end run on me and I Reversed it! Instead of screwing me, he led me to the goose with the golden egg.

Milk Toast

When I was Staff Regional Manager for a correspondence school, a young milk-toast type of guy walked into my office looking for a job in the field of sales. I looked him over and told him this was a pretty rough game. He told me his father was professor at one of the universities. I said he should be a teacher instead, but he insisted that he wanted to be in sales.

Unlike my old nemesis Sweet Willy who only pretended to help people, I really wanted to see this young milk-toast succeed. I saw character in him and admired him for his tenacity.

I told him how the process worked: "You don't have to be a closer. Just follow up on the progress of the students you do enroll. You could beat all the talented closers in the office who use their hit-and run tactics and don't follow their student's progress."

He may not have had the aptitude of a closer, but he had the right attitude which was more important. He did exactly as I said and focused on quality instead of quantity. Long story short, he went on to win a car in a contest, even beating me. Now that's a Reverse.

The Little Boy

Once again the office gave me one of their famous recycled leads, so I went out to a home to see a very upset prospect. When I was face to face with him, he unloaded on me with rage because he had been previously scammed by some salesman who told him that the ditch he bought could be used to launch his yacht. He took it out on me because I was from the same company. After listening to him rant for quite awhile, he finally apologized and explained that he was just so upset about the whole affair. I gave him my card and left, only vaguely aware that his little boy had been in the room the whole time and watched as I calmly listened to his father's complaints.

There's no significance from this story... except many years later I received a call from a guy who wanted to buy a lot from an ad he'd seen in the paper. When I went to his job site to pitch the deal, he wasn't there. I wrote the encounter off, thinking it was just another goose chase. I received a second call from the same guy, apologizing for standing me up. This time we did connect at his job site.

After I sold him a lot, he asked me, "Do you know why I called you?"

"Because you wanted a lot," I said.

"I was a little boy several years ago listening when you came to my home and my father unloaded on you. You were so gracious about accepting the problem for something you didn't do. I never forgot about it. I saw your ad in the paper and I wanted to deal with you."

The truth was I had forgotten all about the incident!

I found out he was a developer, and the next month he bought more lots off me, all because of something I'd done all those years earlier. That's *still* not the end of the story; he went on to purchase even more lots from me after that!

This was all because of something that little boy remembered years earlier. Now is that a Reverse? All because I could take the heat from what some scam salesman did.

The Grubby

This one's for the books: I remember being in a sales office that practiced a concept called "floor time." When a potential prospect walked in, the salesman who gets to pitch him is decided on rotation. One day this guy came in and he looked like he had crawled up out of a sewer. He was a real mess, looked pathetic. The salesman who saw him coming in, even though it was his turn to pitch the next prospect, walked away. Everybody in the office asked the next guy, until the manager decided to dump this grubby guy on me. The truth was, I wasn't thrilled to have to deal with him either, but I knew how to blow out prospects that I did not want to pitch.

I approached the man and he said, "I want to buy some property."

I thought to myself, *Well everybody comes in asking about property - it doesn't mean they're going to buy.*

The grubby guy continued, "I don't want any ocean front property. I want it way out in the back where the storm can't get me."

Maybe you don't get this Reader: waterfront property cost an arm and a leg, and he's telling me he "doesn't want that." He wants the boonies, whereas the average person would want the ocean front property.

Real quick, trying to be polite to get him out of there I said, "Look, I think I can get you a property out in the boonies for a certain price. Can you work out those terms? How's your credit?"

"I don't have any credit," he said. "But I have cash." And he proceeds to pull several thousand dollars out of his pockets! I was surprised to say the least! I wrote the contract and the grubby guy was very happy with the exchange.

When I walked into the manager's office holding all of the money in my hands, he could not believe it! The other salespeople were in disbelief. It was like a gift, but it wasn't supposed to be my gift. I wasn't the next guy in line to pitch him, but I took the opportunity they didn't want. *That's* a Reverse.

In sales, there is only luck, talent, and numbers. This one was luck.

The Screamer

One of the more interesting stories was the time when the light bulb went off in my head with a great strategy on how to sell properties as a win-win to both the prospect and myself. Here's how it happened: I went to make a presentation in a prospect's home. I had another sales rep with me —because he wanted to hear me make a pitch. The prospect was a pretty decent guy, but his wife was a screamer. She was angry because the last guy sold her a boondock lot. Of course we're there, so I became the target of her vengeance. She screamed us right out of the house! We didn't want anything more to do with her.

Now listen to his: a few months later I was down in my basement with no idea where my next deal was going to come from. As I was sitting there in the dark, which I often did, I tried to figure out a plan.

What am I going to do? I thought.

My feet were up on this box of old leads of people who held properties with the company. Many salespeople had the same box of duplicated, recycled leads. In the other sales company, if you remember, I was fired because somebody got a hold of a single duplicate lead.

As I'm sitting on all those leads that I was going to put in the garbage the next day, BINGO – it hits me! Talk about *creating something from nothing!* Wouldn't these people who bought those boondock lots like to pay the same price for a canal lot? I knew the company I worked for was buying canal lots at a low price and selling them at a huge profit. What if I could buy those same canal lots and sell them at a lower price than the company was? I would be doing the prospects a favor by giving them an opportunity to exchange their boondock lot for a canal lot at the same price!

Reader, are you following me so far? So long as the sales company was holding the price up, I was going to look good buying and reselling them for the same price as a boondock lot. Now mind you, I'm still working for the same sales company which means in reality it was a conflict of interest.

I took a trip down to one of these real estate offices looking like a hick from the north and asked the broker, "If I gave you a deposit, could I hold three canal lots for a month? And if I don't come back, you can keep the deposit."

They couldn't believe it. "Three?" they laughed at me. "We'll give you all you want!"

They thought I was a real sucker. I wanted to buy lots from them they felt they were stuck with because they didn't know how to promote them. For all their knowledge about the properties, they couldn't sell them.

I gave the real estate broker my deposit and took the 3 lots. I came back home to my basement and took a lead out of that old box and called a prospect. Over the phone I told her, "I understand that you bought a lot from this sales company some years ago that sits out in the boondocks. What if I told you I could offer you a canal lot for the same price? And I don't even want your boondock lot in exchange."

She said, "Who do you think you're kidding? You can't do that."

I said, "What if I could? Is six or seven a good time this evening to show you?"

She said to come over at six. I went over and simply told her to show me her lot on the map. I then showed her one that sat right on the canal.

I said, "I'll make this deal on a land contract for the same price you paid for your lot."

She couldn't bless me enough. She told her husband over and over what a great deal I had given them. As I left the house, it suddenly occurred to me: she was the screamer! I didn't realize it even when I was pitching her (maybe because she wasn't screaming). Of all the prospects I could have contacted to start this cottage industry with selling canal lots, it turned out to be her. Another Reverse!

That's how it all started. With only a small deposit out of pocket on the lots at the real estate office, I bought the property for about 20 cents on the dollar and resold them at a handsome profit. The prospects had the chance to buy a canal lot at a reasonable price, and everybody was happy. It was a win-win.

At the time, there was a bank president that approached me. He knew what type of guy I was, and asked what I was into. I told him I was promoting canal lots. He asked if we could work a joint venture, and I told him I'd be glad to. He asked me how much financing I needed and I told him I didn't need any financing. Being a bank president, he'd never heard that one before. It was a Reverse from most guys who were always trying to hit him up for a loan.

Instead, I told him I needed prospects.

"I have a lot of connections," he said. "How many prospects do you want?"

I said, "Let's see how many canal lots there are."

Unfortunately, the opportunity was lost. The following week he went on vacation for a month. Meanwhile, the sales office I worked for caught on to what I was doing. They called me into the office to read the Riot Act to me. They wanted to know if I was working against the grain.

"Are you selling these lots at a lesser price?" they asked me.

I looked them in the eye and said, "Absolutely! And if you could get away with it, you'd do it to. Is there anything else you want to talk about?" And I walked out of the office.

Did I keep my job? Of course! I was still their top producer. They weren't stupid like the other company that fired me. This was the same company that was rolling in the aisles laughing in disbelief when the other outfit fired me with their trumped up allegation. Remember they had been trying to pirate me out of there anyway for years.

So I was able, with audacity, to work both deals – my little cottage industry as well as the company. Now, because the bank president didn't come through right away, I lost the time element. My company went out and bought up that entire inventory from the real estate resale office. They bought them for the same price I did and resold them for three times as much as I was selling them for. With the inventory off the market, the deal was over.

When the bank president came back from his vacation and heard the news, he asked me, "Well, can we do it again?"

"No," I said. "It's done."

Time kills. This is why I never wait.

The Prince of Saudi Arabia

At one time I had an appointment to pitch a nephew of the royal family of Saudi Arabia – a prince who was scheduled to come to town. I sold some property to a jeweler who was planning on selling some diamonds to the prince when he arrived. I asked if maybe he'd be interested in some real estate while he was here. The jeweler said he might, and that he would have the prince call me when he visited.

There was a certain property at the office that nobody could sell. It's not that it didn't look good – it was aesthetically beautiful with golf courses, homes, and canal lots connected to gorgeous parks. I was thinking how I could sell him a piece of the property...when it occurred to me I could pitch him *the entire package!* This was a dream offering – a once in a lifetime opportunity. I set up all the paperwork for the meeting. I had it master planned, and I was just wringing my hands waiting for the appointment.

Guess what happened?

Fate stepped in when one of the Saudi family members died that weekend. The prince never reached town. But as I always say, you never lose what you never had... so forget that deal.

The Ringer

At times I put together deals that were too big for one investor alone, so I promoted them as shares in a joint venture. The trick is to get the first prospect involved to buy a share. Why? Nobody wants to be first, so once you do have him you give him an inducement to find the rest of the investors. That inducement might be a First Right of Refusal, which means that if one of the other investors who buys eventually in the future decides to get out of the package, the first guy in has the option to take that share. By having the majority of the shares, he controls the package.

I was putting together this joint venture some time back, and it was like a lock deal. I'd done my due diligence, crossed the t's and dotted the i's. I had everyone qualified. The stakes were high with this particular package, and I in effect did everything I could to pull it off. So I had all the potential investors in an audience and presented the package to them. I could see that everybody was in agreement, and thought it was a done deal.

However….

All of a sudden this guy pops out of the woodwork like a cockroach with a stupid remark which poisoned the minds of the whole audience. It blew them all right out of the deal. Even if there was or was not credibility to his remark, his words were all it took with an audience to kill that deal.

This kind of character is called a ringer. They are just in there to upset the apple cart, and they're very good at it. If you know in advance that a ringer is coming with your group of investors, postpone the pitch.

If you were to pitch the deal, not only will you lose the potential package but it will upset your momentum. You'll feel bad that you lost it and that could destroy you from the next deal you're going to pitch. In other words you're not only *not* taking something from them, but the ringer is taking something from you. That's a Reverse.

The best thing you could do is postpone the presentation and hope he's not there for a repeat performance. Otherwise, *adios* joint venture deal.

"I Don't Like You"

As I said, with these sales types I seldom won the popularity contest. There always seemed to be someone who resented me because they'd heard an alleged remark, something like "this guy's playing some games, he got to be doing something shady." Almost every time when they confronted the issue with me one-on-one, they would realize the truth and apologize to me. In fact, some of them became good friends.

Being a loner, I probably set myself up to these negative remarks. I would not dignify a response to defend myself when these busy bodies came up with accusations against me.

I remember getting a call one day from another salesman. He knew about my track record in the industry, but we had never met personally even though I worked for the same company. He called me saying, "I got your phone number from the office. I heard about you, and I've got to tell you… I don't like you and I really don't know why."

I was overwhelmed by this guy, calling me up out of the blue. I asked who he was and said, "You've never met me, how could you draw any conclusion?"

He said, "I've heard so much about you."

"What did you hear?" I asked.

"That you write a lot of business, and everyone's wondering how you do it."

After talking to him for a while, I came to realize he was a man with a lot of moral backbone. Within 45 minutes he apologized to me and invited me out to lunch. I gladly accepted.

He became one of the best guys I ever met in the business. Later on, he had a chance to become the head of the sales division that sold houses. We both had a chance for this position as housing manager, but I stepped down because I didn't want to compete against him. I personally thought he could do a better job than me in the position.

He got the position but because he did, it built a lot of resentment from other salespeople in the office. Willy and the rest of that crew would dump on him. He took a lot of heat from them, which upset him. At times it seemed I was the only one he could feel some comfort with in that office.

Now remember how this started out, with him calling me on the phone and saying he didn't even like me? In the end, he said I was one of his best friends. Another Reverse.

Lady Charm

One of my many big experiences in sales was the time I chased a lead in a shady part of town. As I came up to the torn screen porch I heard a lady scream, "Down Hitler, down!" This toothless wonder chewing on a pork chop bone swatted her dog for taking a dump inside the house.

As she opened the door, she started apologizing for the garbage that was stacked up in her kitchen, saying, "Oh gee, I've been so busy I just didn't quite get to it today."

It was obvious that much garbage had been stacking up for weeks, making it a feast for any rat.

I immediately excused myself, saying I had left something in the car. I said goodbye to Lady Charm and little Adolf as I Reversed myself out the door. I don't think I suffered any loss there.

<u>The Golden Handshake</u>

There was a time when I had an Englishman and his wife come to my office. I was pitching him a deal and when it was all said and done he still didn't commit to buying.

"I want to think about it," he said. "If I like it, I'll call you later and you will get my golden handshake."

I knew better than that – if I didn't close right then and there at the end of a pitch, usually nothing happened.

Later on that evening while I was in bed I got a phone call. Right away the person on the line said, "You've got the golden handshake!"

"Who is this?" I said, still waking up.

"I'm the gentleman you were presenting your deal to today. I've decided to accept your offer."

"We have a deal then?" I asked. "Come by my office ten o'clock tomorrow and we'll sign the contract."

"Yes," he agreed. "I'll be there."

He came to the office the next day and made a big to-do about shaking my hand. "This is the golden handshake!" he told me excitedly. "Whenever I give a man my promise, I keep my word."

That evening, he called me up again and guess what? He cancelled.

I asked him, "Whatever happened to that 'golden handshake'? Did it turn to rust?"

He didn't respond and hung up. Classy guy.

Sid the Sewerman

Let me introduce you to a character with a hyperbole. For those of you who don't know what that is, grab a dictionary.

Imagine the best closer in the world has just closed on a deal. The prospect is thrilled with the transaction. He goes down the street for a stroll and – by chance – a guy pops up out of the sewer. It's Sid the Sewerman who barely finished the fifth grade and is a friend of the prospect.

The prospect is so excited with the deal that he's just purchased that he says to Sid, "Hey, I just made a great deal!"

Sid, who knows nothing about the details of the sale, wipes away the grime from his face and yells back, "Uh oh! You shouldn'ta dun dat."

In just a few moments of talking he has poisoned the prospect's mind, who now can't wait to call and cancel the deal. Sid, not exactly a pillar of society, has just beaten the most talented closer in the world. Now that's a Reverse!

Here's my point: with all the facts and persuasion of this high-powered sales pitch I'm teaching you, Sid – with a whole lot of nothing – wins the day. It shows you just how fickle a prospect can be, and again proves that emotion can beat logic.

Wimps

How many times does a prospect open his door, and the salesperson standing there says, "I'm not selling anything."

Yeah*, sure.*

Why would you lightweights want to insult the intelligence of the prospect? No wonder the public seems to have this image of salespeople as lowly peddlers. They hardly consider sales as a profession, thinking it's just another pest at the door. Whenever a prospect asked me if I was selling something, I would respond, "Of course I am. That's if you can qualify…"

Personally, I'm sure at the beginning of a pitch they may have even had that image of me. But before I finish that pitch, whether I closed or not, I received their respect. There was no way I'd stay around five minutes if I didn't get it.

For many wimpy salespeople, their first concern was to suck up to the prospect. They were busy kissing the babies and petting the dog as a way to break the ice in a pitch. I doubt they received any respect at the close, which might explain why they didn't sell. The Reverse was I just maintained control and would not do any sucking up. I first had to receive respect, popularity was second. It was always in that order and I generally got them both by the end of the pitch, whether I sold or I didn't.

Reader, why do you think there were so many of these lightweights in sales to begin with? Let me enlighten you: most sales offices ran what they called a body shop. They would do mass recruiting and spin a tail about how much money you could make in sales. They realized it was the old numbers game. After some of the sales recruits wrote their relatives, they would fade out of the business. So sales offices would just keep recruiting, throwing bodies against the wall to see what sticks.

Creative sales can test your mettle. If you can survive rejection, cancellations, depression, and marginal support, you can probably make a good living. Some sales organizations offer a draw for a short time to help new recruits get off the ground, knowing that these sales types will usually offset the draw if they write a deal by selling their relatives or friends. They knew that most of these neophytes will eventually quit anyway. Personally, I would not accept draws because I could pull my own weight in the sales game.

The truth is many people in direct sales do not make enough to pay their bills because they are generally lazy. They compound the problem by using escapism in drinking, smoking, and other types of fooling around so they won't have to admit the truth they were never supposed to be in sales to begin with. They're out all day and night, causing personal problems in their lives.

Many sales quitters complain and rationalize that sales is a bad deal. I know if they were making money they wouldn't be complaining so much. That would be a Reverse. For them to claim that "sales was not for them" hides their real motive which is that they couldn't cut it amid so much uncertainty and rejection. Instead they used a wimpy, trite cop-out statement that sales is not worthy of them. In truth they simply didn't work at it.

It's been my experience that if these lightweights were out into the trenches working instead of whining at the office, they wouldn't crap out so easily. Quitters are usually the same guys who have dried up their draws and been cut off from the spigot. They think that getting the draws from the sales office will help them by giving them more time to close their sales, but it's the Reverse! They become dependent on the draw and then fail to produce, causing them to quit.

The criticism of this type of sales person is not that they won't pay the price of endurance to succeed, but that they're hypocrites about their real motives. They fault the companies and not themselves.

I was willing to help any fellow salesperson when they asked me. I think I was pretty generous at times by splitting deals with other salespeople or giving them part of my commission just to drive me to the prospect's home. It was not a big sacrifice for me to help them out. This was different than when I had to placate the coffee machine crybabies and give them something just to shut them up.

Many times these characters were legally stealing from me anyway because that's the way these companies were set up. If you've got a sales staff who are not writing business and you don't throw them a bone now and then from my deals, they'll go down the street to some competitor with greener pastures.

These sales managers made sure that there was some devious clause in the deal he didn't tell me about when I first hired in (the sin of omission). They would tell me, "Of course, you've got to give a piece to the other rep. It was once his lead."

Yeah, maybe 2 years ago when he first pitched it and couldn't close.

They were not exactly Robin Hood, stealing from the rich to give to the poor. I'm sure in their lives these guys couldn't have been any poorer than I was when I was a kid. If I want to give something to charity that should be my option. But these managers had the formal power to just take it from me. They were generous to the other salespeople at my expense, not theirs.

Reader, if you feel I'm too tough on some of these salespeople, how would you feel if they were in your pocket? Case closed.

True Character

Some prospects were so pissed trying to find the scam artists who sold them a bad deal, it was suggested that they put the salesperson's face on a milk carton with the caption: WANTED DEAD OR ALIVE. These bandits gave a black eye to the rest of us. At the same time, many of the sales managers were just as guilty by association. They turned a blind eye to the dirty deeds perpetrated on the prospects by these slick characters.

When a grief call came in from a prospect who had been lied to by a salesperson, the sales managers would need to offer the prospect some sort of compensation to cool the grief. They would first show an act of dismay, feigning that the sales office did not tolerate that kind of behavior. They assured the prospect that they will certainly discipline the salesperson who did it to them, which gets the office and the salesperson off the hook. Then, behind closed doors, they poo-poo the whole ordeal and allow the same behavior to continue again. They just wanted the deals.

Personally I would never comment to them about this kind of attitude, but indirectly these prospects were thinking that we were all guilty of this behavior. It made closing sales that much harder. Again Reader, you probably also had a negative attitude about salespeople. But these characters were void of *character*.

As for myself, anytime a prospect attempted to get me to defend what these shysters did, I simply Reversed the situation by blowing right by their statement. I would first agree to disarm them from the conversation. Then I would revert by to a query about them. My formula was agree, disarm, attack (in that order). Never argue, never defend.

If any of you salespeople want to know more about my subtle techniques, I suggest you call me for a consultation at 586-873-2987 because these techniques vary from one prospect to another. Certainly it will improve the sales performance of some of you.

Getting back to the office, the other salespeople knew I was not a scam artist and I didn't talk behind their backs. Based on my character I generally had their respect. I would take an interest in them. Those that didn't respect me, I didn't care anyway.

Mind you, I am a product of the 40's and 50's where I started off with little in life, but learned to take on responsibility. In those days, life went like this: you get married, go to college, raise your kids, get more schooling, shoulder your social responsibilities, take the layoffs when they're handed to you, and struggle through. And if you're Catholic you obey the Lenten rules of no eating or drinking during certain times. You've got all this coming at you, and you just *did it*.

The American Dream was not always pleasant; it was tiring and exhausting. When I went into sales, I was considered a very conservative guy because I did not abandon this sense of responsibility that I had been raised with. I was working beside all these sharks who were living large with their commission – whenever they had one – while creditors were chasing them for car payments, alimony and other debts. It was their way of life! Even the national trainer had creditors after him. And as they say, desperate people will do desperate things. I was still my own man no matter what they did.

In sales, nobody cares how close you came to writing a deal – it isn't horseshoes. If you don't close, you don't get paid, and those wolves I mentioned will be at your door all the same. I had the ability to make a very good income out of sales. I had it embedded in my mind that I could not afford the luxury of losing.

After consistently being a winner, I felt I had the baggage of being a champion and had to stay on top all the time. It's an ego trip. When I came in second, it bothered me. I didn't want that kind of headache. Of course nobody can be number one all the time, but it still weighed on my mind. After all, even when you do come in first, it's all over like the snap of your fingers and you start again.

On any given day, somebody else can beat you. That's the truth of it. I could not allow myself to get discouraged so I would worked smarter to Reverse that outcome, and that takes *character*.

The Mystery of the Creative Mind

As a sales driven guy, in my opinion the "glass is always half full." Some crybabies out there will always see the glass as half empty. It's the sad part of modernity when you get attached to all the goodies and you forget how you got them in the first place, by hard work. Now they just want the toys without earning them. Many salespeople have the same problem blaming somebody else if they are not making sales.

Once someone gives in and starts complaining, it's like a virus. It becomes a habit for others to copy. The magic cure for bad habits is good work by salespeople working the numbers – a question of *attitude*.

Some years ago I recorded a tape called *"Personal Commitment: Creative Salespeople versus American Workers."* In it I talked about the A students versus B students. An A student can at times sit on their laurels, generally getting the big job when they graduate, whereas the B student comes in second banana to be hired.

In sales, I can tell you that's a Reverse – the prospect doesn't give a rat's @$$ if you are a scholar. The B student who has his pedal to the metal with the correct attitude will overcompensate by trying harder. Thus the B student will not only catch up with the A student, but may surpass them. The poetic justice is that the A student may end up working for the B student because of his aggressive attitude. Now isn't that's a Reverse?

Just for the record, yes I'm one of those B students. Remember when I discussed a balanced lifestyle with control, where you become a winner? Well that's a byproduct of attitude. The Reverse is that the one with aptitude can be out of control if he doesn't do something, ending up a naval gazer in an ivory tower just living on their laurels.

Of course if one has both attitude and aptitude, they're special. You wrap them up in cellophane. They're the future leaders like Lee Iacocca and Ted Turner. Aptitude is a God-given talent. Attitude is something you develop yourself. My major in college was not psychology, yet it doesn't take an expert to understand this bit of common sense.

Everything I've discussed so far has been contingent on attitude and aptitude. It appears that this society recognizes aptitude more, but to implement a strategy is more about attitude.

The ultimate guarantee of success is not just about talent. It's also about the *numbers*.

Sure, some may say that success is determined by more than just money, but what's the first thing out of most people's mouths? "This guy's a millionaire" or "That person is loaded." Personally I am more impressed by the success of a well-balanced individual with a healthy attitude – someone in sales who treats the prospect with the same respect they want for themselves, regardless if they make a sale or not.

It's been my experience that closers generally lived in the fast lane at the expense of their families with their selfish lifestyle. They were considered a success by how much they produced in sales, but as family men they were disasters.

In sales it's all about your commitment to attitude. You need the stomach to handle rejection. There is one word that can stop most salespeople who cannot deal with rejection, and that word is *no*. With attitude, it keeps you alive until you hear the word *yes*. Especially when you write a deal and the next day the prospect cancels on you due to buyer's remorse. That's the acid test of what a salesperson is made of.

A good attitude means that a salesperson takes on their own responsibility and does not blame others for their setbacks. Once you travel down the road of pointing the finger at someone else, pretty soon you won't have the motivation to get up out of bed in the morning. In fact, each time you condition yourself to blame others, you weaken yourself. If there's blame, start with yourself. Then get over it and start again.

You see, the field of sales is very democratic. It's the only place where everybody has a chance to fail. Imagine reader, you are getting all this wisdom and still only paid the price of a fast food take out. *Lucky you*! If we ever meet, you can thank me by buying me a good meal.

Teach Them How to Lose

Unlike some of my flaky sales managers, I was not in a dream world of sociology where I was in sales "to help people." I feel that kind of attitude is not functional in the sales arena. Neither is relying on academia to teach you the ropes. You can't earn control with just a degree or knowledge; you have to take charge of it to begin with.

In the past, I have trained the trainers who thought that salespeople should hang their hats on just product knowledge. It's not just your aptitude, it's your attitude too. And your attitude isn't correct, you're out of control. And if you're out of control, your competitor is in control and you lose by default.

I want to talk about the apologetics of all this. Once I had conjured up a master plan to sell a deal, I couldn't wait to get out of bed in the morning and implement it. Sometimes my plans worked and other times they didn't. When my plans didn't work, I maintained my momentum by remembering I couldn't lose what I never had. On top of that, I always had a plan B.

Always assume the worst and be ready for plan B if your first plan fails. That's a Reverse. As Robert Burns wrote, *"The best laid plans of mice and men often go astray."* Only a flake would put all their chips on just one plan. Reality tells you that more deals fail than succeed, so you should be prepared to shift gears ASAP.

I initially learned the hard way in sales with all the broken commitments by prospects as well as my office managers. That's when I developed my attitude to assume the worst, because the best always took care of itself.

Every now and then some lightweight sales type, who couldn't close his mouth let alone a sale, would tell me my outlook was too negative. Of course, within a few months this same dreamer would usually check himself out of the business because he could not survive in creative sales. He was possibly a refugee of one of those rah-rah motivational speakers that talked all about being positive, and very little on how to actually close a deal.

I would suggest that motivational speakers teach more on how to lose instead of how to win – another Reverse. Why? Because as I've said, the salespeople encounters the word *no* more than *yes*. I'll bet I will get a lot of flak from some dreamy-eyed psychologist for that statement.

Creative sales can be a heartbreaking business if one cannot accept rejection. If salespeople want to succeed in the sales game, they should be aware from the get-go that setbacks are always just around the corner. If sales motivators really want to help budding salespeople, they should emphasize the hardships not the rewards.

Would you believe that for most sales types just entering sales, the worst thing that could happen is that they close their very first pitch? Why? Because they will get all hyped up thinking it will be easy. The Reverse is that it's better if they fail on their first pitch. That way, they get a lesson on how to deal with the reality of rejection. Rejection can build character and prepare them for a more realistic attitude if they can handle it.

My experience in sales taught me that the illusion of so-called positive thinking is a crock. It does not prepare you for when your bubble bursts. If by chance you are not inner motivated, some salespeople might still just get by. I never saw when positive thinking for salespeople kept their morale up if they were not writing sales – but it just sounds good.

Reality teaches that there are always more setbacks than there are positive events that occur during the trappings of the day. If you do not have a stomach for these situations, you're prepared for failure.

Don't understand me too quickly you textbook techies. Being motivated within kept me focused because I wasn't relying on the unrealistic jabber of some motivational speakers who never accomplished what they preached. They can put you under ether with their presentations on how to sell, but once you're out in the trenches you're back to square one, scratching your head trying to implement what they said.

Let me be clear: I'm not stereotyping all motivational speakers. I am only referring to the ones I personally heard, and I can tell you I didn't make a dime on any of their offered advice. The time they took to give a spiel I could have been back on the street writing a deal.

Speaking of stereotypes, salespeople in general have been given a bad rap. There are so many rip-off artists scamming prospects that many good salespeople are conditioned to think that it's always the prospect who has the high moral ground. Some salespeople start to think that they are lower than plant-life in the prospect's eyes.

Get over it.

You are not responsible for what other shifty salespeople have done. This is the one reason why you are intimidated by the prospect's typical objections, "I don't want to buy, I've been stung before."

Almost every salesperson goes through that in the beginning. I thought the same way until I Reversed my attitude. I realized that the prospect and I were not the bad guys. The prospects I pitched seldom gave me that image. With control, I received their respect and they usually liked me – but in that order.

It's no wonder why salespeople who suck up to the prospect can't make a sale. The prospect knows they're being sucked up to and gives the salesperson little if any respect. They play the game with a weak salesperson with that popularity routine. They're under the impression that since the salesman is such a nice guy, he won't put the bite on them and sell them something. Sound familiar? I left no doubt that I was all about business, not making friends by sucking up.

KennethFGeorge.com – Look It Up

It's been said that there's so much opportunity, no one should be unemployed in this country. But first they have to get off their butts and be a risk taker. With a little bit of training and someone giving them guidance on how to open a storefront, they could be in business in no time.

Even if we were in good times – whether the economy is up or down – the cup is always half-full. You don't depend on the times for your success. You don't wait for things to happen, you make them happen. You don't fill the need, you create the need.

Staying motivated within, I recognized that something good usually came out of all my mistakes and screw-ups. I always looked for the silver lining. When I was a kid, we were short of money so we created our own toys – we created something from nothing. I didn't invent this concept, but I was able to retain it in my sales career where it paid off.

Do you really want to know the secret of selling? Now listen carefully…between me and you, *there ain't no secret*. Get it? No secret.

Yes, I admit some of you may have taken it literally when you saw that phrase come up on my blog www. KennethFGeorge.com – but that's just to get your attention. You're looking for a magic bullet that does not exist. Yes, there are talented techniques used by professional closers. The rest is simple: just work the numbers with control using the law of averages, and you can make a living selling.

As for myself, my technique of the Reverse works for me and for some salespeople with special ability. Not all, however. I can try to train a rock all day long with my Reverse sales closing technique, and it will still turn out to be a rock. Again, no secret.

It's just like some overweight people – with the exception of those with a medical history – who consume enough food for an entire village and say they can't understand why they can't lose weight. All the while they're munching through a box of donuts that the kids will never see, reading a book about the "secret to losing weight." Yeah, *big* mystery. There is no magic bullet. Just close your mouth and the mystery is over. They could keep their insurance premium from going up when God forbid they develop diabetes. At the same time, I had great respect for big people if I saw them at the gym. They weren't looking for a secret, they just worked out hard. That's a Reverse. I admired them for trying to get *control* of their lifestyle and their weight.

I think what the problem is for some of these sales types, just as it is for some of these wide track well fed people, they will not pay the price with discipline. They do not accept that their destiny is in their own hands. Instead they try to avoid responsibility, thinking there's something out there in the cosmos that is the secret of life to solve their problems. In the meantime they blame everything and everybody for their situation.

The fault lies not in the stars dear Brutus, but in ourselves."

Reader, are you impressed with my classical Shakespearean quotes? Whatever! Let's move on to the actual blog posts from my website…

Attention Struggling Salespeople

There now is a successful, unique method available to closing sales. It is taught by an award-winning expert who has trained the trainers in the process we call The Reverse. You've tried it all your way – not happy? Now try it my way.

Get Smart, Get Me.

Why Aren't You Closing More Sales?

What if I told you that you could create something from nothing?

What if I told you, you can never lose?

Let me give you one big reason why you aren't closing more sales: the prospect can predict your pitch!

Why?

Because he has basically heard it all before, which puts him in a position of control. And if he's in control you, my friends, are out of control.

The prospect maintains this control by using a defense mechanism of objections onto you which forces you to defend your product or service. Street smarts tells you to never defend. It is suspect.

As in Shakespeare's Macbeth, "Me doth think the lady protests too much;" defending.

For the salesperson to have control and not the prospect, instead of disagreeing he should first agree (which is a reverse!), then disarm, and then attack.

This unique philosophy of overlapping techniques and concepts is what I call......"The Reverse."

The Reverse is not just some razzle-dazzle idea that some pitchman showers on his audience, which can put them under ether. Once back in the trenches, salespeople don't know how to implement the razzle-dazzle idea that been said by the speaker, putting them back to square one.

The Reverse is a process I personally developed with great success in my own career. I have consulted with various sales organizations who implemented this Reverse process also with great success.

This program is not taught anywhere else in the country.

In addition to learning how to create something from nothing, you will learn how to never lose. I will show you using all these different techniques of numbers/ time/

momentum/ character/ characters/ personal commitment, etc. I will show you how aptitude/attitude on how all these concepts interlock with The Reverse.

I will explain in great detail the numerous closing techniques during a pitch and how you – the salesperson – will control leading to the close.

I will tell you that in my experience, the best pitch may be the shortest pitch. In addition, I will cover topics of momentum/ loss of confidence/ grief calls/ two-call closes/ time, timing, and tone/ decision-making/ role-playing, and competitors. I will talk about master plans/ conceptual frameworks/ luck, talent, and numbers, and the phone being friend or foe.

I will tell you about never thanking the prospect.

All of this in sales philosophy interacts with The Reverse.

I'm well aware that it's a tough economy with maybe 20% unemployed – but remember, if 20% are unemployed, that means 80% are still prospects.

Remember above all, you will have success through personal commitment.

My future blogs will explain this unique philosophy of the Reverse, so stay tuned and you will understand this concept of the Reverse, which will allow you to increase your sales production with this sales savvy.

I can show you how to bump your sales production possibly 30% a year using The Reverse.

Control: The Key to the Close

Hello. Are you still with me?

Class begins. Great!

In my previous post, I said control is the key to the close using my unique concept of The Reverse.

If the prospect can predict the presentation, he is in control. If he's in control you, my friends, are out of control. Get it?

Now, let me ask you a question: When does control begin?

Almost every sales rep attending my seminars said, "It begins as soon as the pitch does." Right?

Wrong!

Why? Because you are on the prospect's turf and he is usually confidently already in control, not you. It's at most a 50-50 shot that you will take control, and I don't like those odds. Allow me to burst your bubble. You were taught that control begins as soon as you start your pitch. Not your fault.

The answer: control has to begin before you leave the post. Get it? Before the pitch, not during (this is a reverse!).

Of course, you have to maintain control during the entire pitch as well. Once a sales rep understands that you can never lose what you never had, and really accepts this idea, he will be relieved of personal pressure and intimidation.

Now you can go to your pitch already in control. No matter the outcome, your ego is still intact whether you close or you don't. You will still have your momentum with no loss of confidence, prepared to take on the next prospect.

If you lose your confidence, you might as well stay in bed. But with control, you're still prepared to take on the next prospect. Why? Because many sales reps are so overwhelmed by hearing the word NO and all of that rejection that they simply quit.

Now there's no magic pill here. It'll take a few pitches to train your mind to this reverse control concept. If I'm wrong, what have you lost? But what if I'm right?

I wasn't a National Sales Champion by being a flake. I know what I'm talking about.

As I continue into future blogs, I will explain how the Reverse will be used with several interlocking techniques and concepts that are part of my sales philosophy. I can tell you, when I made a sales presentation, I had control with commitments which led me to the close. Many prospects would either lie or buy.

I always prefer a win-win situation, but if there had to be a loser it was always going to be the guy across the table, not me. Sale or no sale.

Why? Because as a salesperson with a family to support, I could not afford the luxury of losing. So I made sure that the prospect would suffer the loss...but carefully so as not to blow up any bridges. If any of you are thinking that this attitude is not the path to popularity with the prospect, let me tell you I was not interested in popularity contests. I wanted respect and usually earned it. Winning the popularity contest with the prospect came as well, whether I closed or I didn't. Respect, then popularity, but only in that order.

Pay attention! What you're hearing from me now you may never hear again.

Stay tuned, you haven't heard anything yet. Remember, this is the Reverse. If it affects you as off-the-wall, imagine what it did to the prospects and what it could possibly do for your sales career!

Control and Pressure

Hello, still with me? Turn off Archie Bunker and finish your beer. Now follow the yellow brick road. There is salvation.

First let's review my previous blog post about my key to the close: this is an epiphany for you lightweights. Control is the key to the close via my Reverse philosophy. It begins before you leave the post, not at the beginning of the pitch. It relieves personal stress knowing you can never lose what you never had.

Okay, now you're engaged with the prospect and want to look professional wearing your three-piece suit and alligator shoes, sporting a pinky diamond ring. Right?

Think again, dreamer.

You are out to impress Mr. Prospect that you are an expert. Right again? Now you're beginning to qualify the alleged "decision maker" with your dog-and-pony show. You're breaking the ice by sucking up, kissing the kids, and petting the dog as you start to overcome the prospect's mundane objections.

Possibly your sales manual gave you so much power it could show you how to sell Girl Scout cookies.

Of course, the prospect thinks he's in control. He happens to be a confident, pipe-smoking engineer-type. He's already told the missus to stay in the kitchen and finish cooking his meal while he uses his logical mind to deal with the peddler. Really?

Now the action begins with the battle of the wits. The salesperson has been taught, "If you can fill a need, you can be successful."

Okkkkay.....surprise! Could there be another way?

And certainly he wouldn't think of putting pressure on the prospect or he could lose the popularity contest. He certainly wouldn't want that to happen.

Gimme a break!

But I haven't mentioned yet this could be a referral lead, which some salespeople define as a lay down (automatic sale). So Mr. Salesman is assuming this is a deal, not just some recycled garbage lead that has already been pitched. He's already counting the gold in his pocket from the commission, and still sucking up to the prospect.

Remember my first blog post? There I stated that the Reverse is made up of interlocking concepts and techniques consisted of: emotion, logic, dividing and conquering, aptitude and attitude, commitment, character, master plan, conceptual framework, competition, & luck, talent, and numbers.

Do you really think Mr. Salesman is aware of any of the above? Call me, and stay tuned for me to connect the dots for you, Mr. Salesman. Either that or you can stay numb-and-dumb with the rest of the sheep, wimping that the world's against them.

The Truth about Recruiting

Sales mentors are useless.

Get this – what you were taught by your so-called "mentors" was like going to war shooting blanks. What you learn through The Reverse Sales Technique here is like going to war loaded for a bear. In my seminars I've heard the statement several times that, "If only I'd known this stuff before I might be driving a Mercedes instead of a Chevy."

Don't use logic in your sales pitch.

This Reverse philosophy is so powerful because there's no way the prospect can logically say no so easily. The reason? He can't honestly know what you're pitching until you, the salesman, tell him. That only happens when you use emotion to make your presentation, not logic. How….??
Follow my blog for more on the answer (that's if you want to

get the jump on the lazy whiners who just talk and grumble, sucking up air).

I never lose whether I make a sale or not.

How's that possible? Call me now – I can educate you in a few hours which will benefit your life more than some college degrees that were supposed to guarantee your future. Right? I will reveal simple techniques that are so disarming that the prospect can never control the situation. Believe me. I'll show you how I used the truth as a tool. My presentations were at least pure as car ads that implied when you purchased a certain automobile you could always get the beautiful model with it. You get my meaning.

Many times sales managers recruited salespeople, telling them what a great opportunity was in front of them. What they were really doing was throwing bodies against the wall and seeing what stuck. And after the salesperson possibly sold a relative, they were under the illusion that they would make the big money. However, many times, that was the end of their sales career. The manager would just recruit another batch of neophytes. Even if the manager knew how to close himself, many times he didn't bother to invest any more time with the salesperson after they'd probably sold their relatives.

The Reverse is a weapon, as I stated earlier, that's not taught anywhere else. How do I know? I invented it! This is not a get-rich at any time scheme, it is simply a unique method that I evolved into by selling. My "mentors" were not any sales manual or manager. Believe it or not, it was the prospects who taught me. As I said before, stay tuned for Sales 101.

The Lazarus Salesperson is Raised from the Dead!

The Reverse pitch is similar to a chess game where at times you can checkmate without going through all the usual moves. How? Check my website. The salesperson already knows the obvious objections and can overcome them with unique strategies. He secures commitments that can neutralize the logic of most prospects. How? Call me. Hint: can emotion be stronger than logic? Here's a bone for you Mr. Salesman – you may have an ally right in front of you. If you don't know who, figure it out.

Listen to me salespeople, you don't have to throw up the white flag and surrender. I have turned around many salespeople from sailing a failed ship called the Titanic, onto a luxury liner of success. There is more to the presentation than just qualifying and overcoming objections to get to the close. Open your ears. There are numerous commitments that get you to the close. If you are floundering, it's because you were trained by the book which states: go step-by-step to cover the basics. In good times, you possibly made a good living using the standard pitch. But you can't live on yesterday's laurels. Today you must be creative and think out of the box. I will show you the way out of the darkness into the light.

Character in Sales

Let's stop. Take a deep breath. Yes, I can explain to you the function of the Reverse, but there's an ingredient that I doubt was ever explained to most of you. It is called character. Without it, you are a machine that needs lubrication.

Character is the stuff that I think separates the winners from the losers. There are many barracuda sales types that can close, but because they lack this quality of character, they will generally say or do anything to put the prospect on paper. They're usually filled with personal and financial problems in and out of the office. Let's put it this way, these are the lowlifes of the sales industry that tarnish the reputation of most salespeople.

Character rises to the occasion whenever there are the usual setbacks.

If you are really serious about what I mean by character, then call me.

Ignorance is not necessarily bliss. So quit hiding behind it as a wimpy excuse. It's not acceptable. Salespeople who would justify the excuse of "I didn't know" are ignorant. Not because they in fact "don't know," but because when told they do not listen. They lack character.

In future blogs, I will show you the relationship of character to recriminations, communications, commitment, etc. If you think I'm being redundant, then you must remember I stated before that the Reverse philosophy is made up of overlapping techniques and concepts. Stay tuned for the next chapter!

Forrest Gump Effect

Snap out of your lethargy and listen! All of you auto workers, put away your crying towels and reject all your gloom-and-doom buddies down at the pool hall. There is salvation. There is a silver lining to build a new career in the field of sales or small business with perhaps little of your buyout money. Now don't blow off this idea too quickly; probably every successful salesperson or small business owner started just that way and never regretted it.

The fact is, the world doesn't owe you anything.

You owe it to yourself, and your family, to pick yourself up with a new career. Here's your opportunity to be a man, and step up into a new career. Why? Because the wolves are still at the door with obligations you have to pay. This is one possible way to honor your personal commitments.

Even in this market, as I stated in an earlier blog, with 20% out of work, there are still 80% that are still potential prospects. This is not rocket science. As I understand, 80% is greater than 20%. And if you can't figure that math out, have your five-year-old figure it out for you.

You can control your own destiny with very little out of pocket. My concepts are unique and simple. It's not a question of smoke-and-mirrors. What is required is a positive attitude called character. Your family is counting on you. The fact is, if some little guy just off the boat can be successful here in America, what could your excuse possibly be? We call this "The Reverse."

Believe it or not, right now you have just a good of a chance in this economic climate of being successful as you had in good times. Why? "Forrest Gump Effect." If you don't get it, call me. I will educate you, because as long as you're vertical there is still hope. People constantly ask me, "When are things going to return back to normal?"

Listen closely, I have a message for you: this IS the new normal! Get smart, and get me.

Salvation for Your Sales Force

Had enough with sales trainers teaching the same old rah-rah sessions with the same old results? To survive you have to be unique in this brave new world. I'm sure you don't need me to tell you that you have to get more creative and start thinking outside the box in these hard times. Do yourself a favor, and allow me to spend a few hours with your sales staff. I'll expose them to the unique philosophy of sales called "The Reverse." It will give them the confidence to control the sales pitch whereby they never lose. The training is informal and powerful. I will demonstrate simple techniques faster and more functional than most high-priced sales organizations with their razzle dazzle.

Now possibly these old methods worked in good times, but today's another story. You can't live on your laurels, and nobody cares what you did yesterday. It's all about "what you've done for me lately?"

I don't want to talk to any of your closers if you should have a couple. They don't need me. And I don't want to talk to your lightweight neophytes at the bottom. They are out of their league and just taking up space which is immoral because they can't make a living to feed their families in this competitive arena. Let them return to a regular 9 to 5 job where it's safe.

However, I can pump up all the reps in the middle who've had some kind of sales production. Mr. Sales Manager, you might be surprised just how many of these people, with just a few of my concepts, could turn into potential closers. Call me at   1-586-873-2987. My informal training of 3 to 4 hours could possible change your bottom line with my top-line techniques using the Reverse philosophy. You can afford me. In fact, you can't afford not to call me.

If I'm wrong, what have you lost? But, what if I'm right?

Salespeople: The Benefactor

Let me set the record straight, Mr. and Mrs. Prospect: there seems to be an attitude among many of you that you are somehow superior to the lonely salesperson. That's probably because you're sitting at an office with your 9 to 5 job, hiding behind your desk. Well let me clue you in, it's a Reverse!

The fact is, whatever you produce in product or service is worthless inventory if not sold by some salesperson.

And if not sold, your employers has no more use for you. Now put that in your pipe and smoke it.

So, Mr. and Mrs. Salesperson, lift up your heads and be proud of your profession, for you in fact are the prospect's benefactor. Ignore the blue suede shoes who gave your profession a bad rap at some time. You're not responsible for them.

Another fact is the salesperson has to be creative every day of his life and is only paid if he closes a sale. You in turn, Mr. Prospect, are paid whether or not you produce anything at all, as you sit with your long coffee breaks talking about your latest golf scores. This in turn forces the company to put you on time-and-a-half of what you don't complete on straight time....ultimately, screwing the stockholders.

Now Mr. and Mrs. Prospect, that you've been straightened out, give respect to the salesperson who is just trying to make a living like yourself. Class dismissed.

Goals vs. Results

I'll bet even money you salespeople have been taught the word goals. Now allow me to tell you struggling salespeople what I think about the word goal. To me, goals can be a convenient excuse for some salespeople to quell their conscience for their mediocre production. In other words, a cop-out.

You see, it doesn't matter how close you come to closing a deal. Now listen carefully. It is not horseshoes. Unless you make a sale, you cannot pay the bills.

So what is the answer?

Write this down: it's called results. So good people, quit talking about goals and just show me the results. Results is what the Reverse philosophy is all about. Call me and I will retrain you brain and explain to you in great detail how to use the Reverse to get your results.

Metamorphosis

Hope you have pencil and paper, I don't intend to keep repeating myself if I can help it. Those of you in sales and marketing who have been following my blogs have been getting a real sales savvy education. However, if you did pay close attention, you realize I usually manage not to complete the puzzle on purpose. Why? I want you to call me to get the whole story on the Reverse philosophy.

Take me up on this opportunity to learn about a new career with sales training that is a step above talking about success stories from a sales trainer who possibly read it from a book instead of in the trenches. Personally, I have lived my strategies and they work. For the price of possibly one night at the casinos, you could invest in a few hours in my program. You may come out a wiser person and metamorphose into a new life.

Guarantees vs. Opportunities

Quit laughing and making racial slurs about immigrants and their small businesses. Their work ethic is commendable, consisting of 12 to 18 hours a day. They put on a clinic everyday of their lives. Nobody gave them anything except the opportunity to feed their families. On the other hand, the American worker wants guarantees. Now let me ask you something: who is still working and who is not? So much for guarantees versus opportunities. This is called a Reverse - get it? However, the immigrant does have something in common with salespeople; neither of them have a union to support them and are only paid if something is sold.

Wise up all you people who lost your so-called guarantees. I would like to show you also that there is still opportunity for those of you who are still risk-takers by trying a new career in the field of sales, where the sky is the limit!

The Glass is Half Full

Laid off? Try the field of sales. "The Reverse" will teach you more about the key to closing deals than most of you have ever been taught by any of your so-called mentors. Here's a fact: as soon as a salesperson makes a sale (now listen carefully) he is unemployed. My point is that anyone who is unemployed is in the same situation as a salesperson. The difference is the salesperson starts work ASAP.

This blog is really about character, which I alluded to in past blogs. The glass is half full for those with character. So what excuse do you have? I know it's tough out there; there are other people who are at least finding part-time jobs or, better yet, creating small business jobs. Others are going into sales where there's always opportunity in a market economy.

The world owes you nothing. Give up the whining at the local bar and change your life. Allow me to train you in a new career in the field of sales.

If you know anything about your American history, then you should know that the revolution was not just about taxes, but ultimately about freedom. I don't know many occupations that allow you more freedom than the field of sales. However, it is a sword with a double edge. Salespeople should use freedom (which is time) more wisely. I say this because the more time that one has, the more time they are apt to waste. However, the reverse is: if one has limited time, it seems the more efficient they are.

Get smart, get me @ 1-586-873-2987

I am available for group seminars as well as personal consultations.

The Clock is Ticking

I wrote this book but the Reverse is I don't consider myself a writer because I don't wait for details. I plunge right in to a project and generally I don't wait for anything or anyone. I worked the numbers by consistently getting one page done at a time. Remember: time is limited, but numbers are infinity.

This ties in with another important concept in sales –the importance of luck, talent, and numbers.

To discuss sales strategy one must understand that luck plays both ways in sales. It's a sword with a double edge – it can work for you or against you.

How often have you heard from the many people who say they're unlucky? On the other hand, if a salesperson gets lucky it's like newfound money. With the law of averages, the numbers will eventually work for you. The harder you work the luckier you get. But so many salespeople whine, waiting for luck to happen, as a cop-out.

In this country, the sky is the limit for the creative salesperson. The opportunity for anybody with the drive to be successful is always a possibility. Numbers strip away the excuses for not at least making a living in the sales game.

The dumbest guy on the planet, with numbers, can achieve a fair degree of success. The problem may be that in this cradle-to-grave society salespeople often feel that knocking on doors is beneath them. With that attitude, they negate the greatest opportunity that the field of sales provides.

The next part of the equation is talent. In reality, only a few really possess the talent to make it to the top. They are the closers; the ones who pump in the volume at many sales organizations. Closers perform well with an impressive batting average of closing most leads that they pitch.

Usually the office managers put the leads in their hands. However it's been my experience that most closers do not go knocking on doors like the average sales reps. In other words, most of the time the closers with talent sit and wait for prospects that the office generates for them, while the average sales rep who may not have talent goes out and works the numbers.

My track record was with my own creative ideas. I rarely waited nor did I want the sales managers to lay leads in my lap. Why? There was always a price to be paid when they wanted a piece of my action. To me, that was a hook in me preventing me from doing my own thing.

Whenever I was conceiving my next master plan, I was concerned I couldn't top the success of my previous deal. Then I realized the simplest thing to do was tweak what I'd done successfully in the past by maybe 5% and I had my new plan! This was a Reverse from most salespeople who tried to reinvent the wheel each time they needed a new plan. I have always done things simple, because simple works.

My best years in sales were generally the recession years. If there were 20% unemployed, there were still 80% still working. The reason why this worked for me was because when things were that bad much of my competition would whine about all the unemployment. They would feed into the negative attitude and quit saying, "Nobody has any money to buy anything." Like Forrest Gump, I was generally the only game in town.

Remember this: deals are either luck, talent, numbers, or a combination of the three. Luck is just great if on any given day it works for you. Talent is self-evident. But anybody who works well with the numbers will not only equal the talented closer, but in reality could pass them up. With all of this said, what possible excuse could any aspiring salesperson have for not making a living? The only gauntlet for salespeople is running the numbers.

When you're talking about sheer numbers, reaching even a small percentage of an audience is significant. If I only reach 5% of my audience with this book, and they pick up one or two techniques, it may increase their sales volume significantly by possibly as much as 30%. Then I know both you and I will have succeeded.

Working the Numbers

One source of leads I had that everyone had was the *Yellow Pages*. On one occasion while looking for leads, I was simply thumbing through the Yellow Pages when it occurred to me to make a phone call. So I blindly opened up a page, landing in the produce section. I called the very first number on that page and asked for the manager. When he was on the line, I talked to him like I was a regular shopper at his place of business.

Like old friends, I started with the phrase, "Haven't seen you in a while." The merchant pretended he knew me too. People in business are never going to say "I don't know you" because it makes them look bad. They have to say "Aw, yeah, I remember when you came in here, yeah…" They're stuck with their own commitment.

I said, "I remember you had a sale on produce last time I was there. Anyway look, we haven't talked to each other in a long time. I'm with a recreational land company now that has a unique offering. I'd like to drop by this evening between 6 or 7 to present it, what's better for you?"

He reluctantly told me he was a busy guy, but that he would be there. I arrived, wrote two sales, and left happy. He in turn couldn't thank me enough for giving him this good investment, and offered me a referral where I made a third sale. All of this started because I picked his number randomly out of the yellow pages. *That's* creating something from nothing.

Here's one that's good enough for Hollywood: I was pitching a prospect in my office to buy a lot. He was very polite and said he wasn't interested because he had bought one in the past. About 2 or 3 minutes after he left, there was a rap on my door. I thought it was the prospect coming back because he had forgotten something. A different guy opened the door and said, "I didn't mean to be eavesdropping, but do you have any more of that inventory available?" I couldn't sell the guy in the door, but I sold the guy outside the door – another Reverse!

Now here's another one for the books – there was the night when I had a terrible headache. I was in bed tossing and turning for hours and no matter what I tried I could not shake the headache. Then it occurred to me *out of nowhere* how to win the national sales contest. The whole plan was in my head instantly. The contest was already 2 months old, with only 10 days left and the front runner had a HUGE lead. I got up early the next morning, already knowing what I had to do.

Within 10 days, I wrote 44 separate transactions, each of them at least 1 lot. I took the lead in the contest. When I went to the convention where they announced the winner, I was told I came in second behind the salesman who was originally leading the contest. I knew that numerically I had won that contest, and something fishy was going on.

Sure enough, several months later it came out that the winner had been picked as a political decision because he was a minority. His manager had been writing deals in his name, which was illegal. By then it didn't matter, it was done. It was another episode of people finding a way to steal from me. However, I didn't end up doing too badly seeing as I made some extra cash that month from all the deals I had written.

Reader, you might be asking why I would stay in the sales game with all this crap was going on? The answer is that's where the money was. I wasn't allowing anyone to drive me out of the game.

Creating Something from Nothing

I remember when Christmastime came around when I was nine years old, there was a man at the street corner who sold Christmas trees. With a quarter in my hand, I went up to him and asked if I could buy a tree. He laughed at me and said, "Don't bother me."

After an hour passed, he had no more buyers. Instead of then selling me a tree, he lit a match and set the trees on fire right in front of my eyes. Great guy, eh?

When he walked away, I salvaged some branches from the fire and dragged them home with me. I took some rope and tied them around a burnt-out stump of a tree. Not only did I have my Christmas tree, but I got to keep the quarter as well. It was the first time I created something from nothing. It was an indication of what my station in life would eventually become in sales.

Now Reader, did you really think that I had some magic hocus-pocus when I said I could create something from nothing? However, I think I did the next best thing to it. The "something" was always there for all to see – I simply implemented it. Follow the bouncing ball to get educated:

At times when doing seminars or consulting I'd ask my audience if they thought it was important to fill the need of the prospects. Almost everyone said yes. I said it's not important to fill the need, it's more important to *create* the need, which is *creating something from nothing*. When you fill a need you have to wait for someone to ask you for something, and meanwhile your waiting family could be starving. When you create a need, they're eating three meals a day. It's a Reverse.

How do you create something from nothing? One of the most classic ideas I've pulled off was my ad book. Why an ad book? For a closer like myself the only thing that kept me away from having a good year was not having enough prospects to pitch. If I could be in front of enough potential prospects with my batting average, I would have been going to the bank quite often.

However, at times in sales you have dry spells where you don't have any prospects to talk to. So the idea came to me one day to set up an ad book. My plan was to go to merchants and ask if they wanted to advertise in an ad book for a certain price.

To start the ad book I added dummy ads because I knew nobody was going to want to be the first guy in. I went down the street door to door from one shop to the next, asking if merchants wanted to advertise in the book. Of course I failed to mention that I put my own ad in there, which was the biggest sheet in the ad book. So now every time I made a presentation, I was in front of a possible prospect.

After talking to maybe 10 or 15 merchants, I had maybe a few of the ads sold. But then one of the merchants took an interest in *my ad*. Upon looking at it he asked me, "Is it possible for me to buy those lots at that price?"

I said, "It's your lucky day, there just happens to be five lots available."

That day, I made a handsome commission from writing that merchant on the deal.

After I accomplished my mission, I went back to the other merchants who had bought ads and returned their money, telling them I couldn't complete the project. They in turn were so impressed because I returned their money. They'd had been ripped off before on other ad books, and thanked me for my honesty.

This temporary ad book was very successful in creating something from nothing – a simple idea that paid off.

Creating something from nothing gave me a mental rush to know I was able to create a master plan that is out there for everybody to see, yet they seem blind to the possibilities of forging them into a saleable concept to present to the prospect. I suspect that most salespeople thought there was much more to putting together a plan. I only knew that I saw everything with a simple approach. I jumped over details and went straight to the big picture first. Then I went back and took care of the details. The Reverse was most salespeople got stuck with paralysis by analysis, wasting time working on the details to get to the big picture. While they're thinking, I'm doing.

These ideas seemed to come easy to me, even as a kid. The reason why I think is because I wasn't afraid to be wrong with these concepts, which were at times off the wall. Rarely was I influenced by other opinions. I was not afraid to think outside the box. I wasn't a follower. If I was, the whole idea of creating something from nothing would have been just a myth.

My Own Man

Eventually the companies were pushing the prices of the properties so high that sales were getting lean. So I faced reality of going into business for myself as a broker. I went to school to get my broker's license. As a broker I was a one man band with no support from anybody. I prepared my own master plan, financed my own deals, and took my rewards as well as my setbacks.

I made several times more as a broker than I ever did being the #1 salesman for any of the land sales companies I had worked for. I could create all kinds of deals without any restrictions from a company. I could wheel and deal at will!

Much like the canal lots I had bought earlier in my career, I could now buy properties on the secondary market for a low price and re-sell them. I was buying the average property for half the amount and selling it back to prospects for a fair price which was much lower than what the sales companies were selling them for. It was a win-win for the prospect as well as myself.

In the meantime, the land deals dried up at the companies for Willy too, so he went to get his own brokerage license. He tried the test three times, but was never able to pass it.

Years later after we'd both left the company, Sweet Willy came to my brokerage office. He dumped a pile of old leads on my desk. If you had seen it come out of a paper basket, you wouldn't have known the difference!

He proposed a partnership, saying, "I want to split any deals you write out of this." He acted like he was making a great concession to me. Sweet Willy, still the scam artist I remembered.

The truth was he couldn't write them himself and he wanted to salvage anything he could out of me if I scored a deal. The fact was if I made any sales he wouldn't have known the difference. He knew that when he dumped them on me, but like always I wouldn't let on. We continued to play the game. It was much more fun than calling him out. If I had said, "Willy, who are you kidding? Get this garbage off my desk!" then the game would have been over.

I didn't know if I could write anything out of that pile, but I did end up writing a few deals out of it. When I split the profits with Willy, he was shocked. I had kept my commitment to share the profits with him – something I doubt Willy would have done for me.

Over the phone, I said to Willy, "I have a check for you."

"*Nyeh, nyeh?*" he whined. "A check? *Nyeh*, what's that for?"

"For the deals we agreed to split." I gave him the check and made no issue out of it. I didn't say what was really going through my head, *Yeah you scam artist, you didn't think anybody could write anything out of that pile of garbage, did you?*

That's what bothered Willy about me – I never showed him any emotion either way. I never played up the fact that I knew he was a scam artist. I just went along with it.

Of all the people I met all those years, Willy was a classic. Everyone needs a Willy to compete against in business, forcing them to be the best they can be.

The Banks

As a broker, I was called on to do seminars for a particular bank where it was obvious that they were watching pennies but losing serious dollars. I noticed that some of the bank tellers were making mistakes by blowing away big depositors with their impersonal attitude. It was so obvious to me. I was thinking, *If they only knew they're passing up these depositors!*

If I was a financial planner for the bank banging on the phone all day, and someone could tell me how just correcting some obvious errors that the clerks were making the bank's financial picture could be substantially increased, I would certainly want to listen.

So I sat with one of their financial planners one day and explained to him this strategy: retirees are always calling in and asking for the current bank rate because they're thinking about extending their CDs. These clerk are picking up the phone chewing their bubble gum, and putting the retirees on hold while they defer to somebody else. The retiree gets impatient and goes down the street to deposit their money in the lap of a competitor's bank.

The point is the clerks have to be informed that this attitude is losing the bank potential deposits. Picking up the phones should be a function that goes directly to the financial planner, not the clerks. This is the same situation I saw while I was in land sales. If you were to fumble away just one or two of these alleged CD depositors, at the end of the year it would have been a significant difference to the bottom line.

I personally know a retiree who is a great example of this. If you burn him because he may not look polished enough when he comes up to a teller, and a clerk even so much as sneers at him or roll their eyes, they've lost his accounts. He'll go up the street and dump *all* his money in another bank. He's just one. Now compound that with all the clerks in the bank who do these things quite often, and then count all the different bank branches you have around where that could happen.

It's such a simple thing that in sales I could see it based on how prospects treated me and how I reacted to them. A simple thing like rolling your eyes or snapping your gum, looking like you're indifferent to a prospect because you think he's insignificant, can lose you a deal. I pointed out this fact while consulting with the bank's financial advisor, who said he saw it happening and didn't even realize it because it was too obvious.

While the financial planner was on the phone trying to find new prospects who wanted a CD, prospects who already have CDs were calling in and getting blown off by clerks with indifference. Now that's a Reverse. They were chasing pennies when the dollars were right in front of them. And every bank seems to do it.

Seminar

Whenever I did a seminar, I never wanted to deal with an office's top salesmen – they're the closers who think they "know it all" with a cocky attitude. They are among the naysayers. At the same time, I don't want to deal with anybody on the bottom who can't close to save their lives – they shouldn't have been in sales to begin with. It's immoral because they can't feed their families and should go back to a 9 to 5 job where it's safe with a weekly paycheck.

For the salespeople who are in between – those than can write some business – I felt I could help boost their sales if they had the desire and some talent to succeed in the sales game.

Some time ago I did a seminar for a prominent insurance company. They had been number one in their division the previous year, but now they were down. I noticed that as I began to speak they acted indifferent, as if I was presenting just another rah-rah motivational speech.

"What's your definition of a successful creative salesperson?" I asked them. I received several different answers. I told them very humbly, "I don't know much about your company – you all know more about insurance than I do. However I do know this: if you're coasting and sitting on your laurels, in all deference to you, if I was your competitor I would come in like a thief in the night and eat your lunch."

Now they were listening and focused on me. I continued, "You must have eternal vigilance and assume the worst because the best will take care of itself. If I was your competitor, you wouldn't get much sleep at night because I would go after your accounts.

"Nobody cares what you did yesterday. It's all about 'what have you done for me lately?' Whenever you stop knocking on doors or banging on phones, you're out of control. If your competitor is doing these things, *they* are in control. Your competitor may not just be the fellow down the street who will pirate your accounts, but possibly the guy across the big pond, possibly the far East. Yes, if you read Thomas Friedman's "The World is Flat," then you realize that the world is smaller due to communications technology in the 21st century. This is no longer the 50's when everything was structured with loyalty to God, family, country, and job. Now competition will get even tougher. If you do not maintain your accounts and take them for granted, you *will* lose them.

"You can't be sitting in your office playing boss with coffee breaks and long lunch hours, hoping your world is at peace. Don't think your boss is your buddy. Remember this: if your boss is taking heat from *his* boss, he will eventually give you a choice to either perform or leave.

"Ultimately you have a moral obligation to your company to be the best you can be. So get creative, create something from nothing, cover your butt, bang on the phone, knock on doors, and allow the law of averages to work the numbers for you. Skip the coffee breaks and the long lunch hours. Get to the gym so you can be physically fit to help you be financially healthy. Generally speaking, nobody fires you, you fire yourself.

"You can't have your feet on the desk, shuffling paper. The money is in the trenches, not the office. When you come out of the ether, whining, and trying to play the blame game as to why your accounts have been pirated out from under you, the answer will be in your own mirror. To not stay on the ball is to disarm yourself and serve your competitor well. He will have it in second gear while you're still in neutral. You have a choice: start hustling or get left at the post. This may be your wake-up call. Stop living on your laurels and go to work."

The audience of salespeople were now wide-eyed as they listened to me. I continued, "Training, skill, and knowledge of products will not necessarily help you close a sale. If knowledge alone did sell, then I'd ship the local library of books onto your lawn. In the end, all you would have is a messy lawn. Let me quote, 'If a little bit of knowledge is a dangerous thing, then who among us has nothing to fear?'

"Prospects don't buy the product, they buy *you*. The product becomes the byproduct, and you become the sale. No matter what our station in life is, we are all salespeople when we promote our products or ideas to others. But to be successful, we must first be creative by selling ourselves. I believe that from beginning to end, a successful creative salesperson must have a personal commitment consisting of aptitude as well as attitude to be on top of their game."

Never Accept Closure

Even though I closed my brokerage office years ago, I have never accepted closure. The adrenaline is still flowing in me. I'm still active. Not one of those old bandits is still at it to the best of my knowledge – another Reverse. Without that good feeling of closure, I'm still active which is obvious by my writing this book!

When you're creating something from nothing, no matter what the situation you must always take something from it. Build on it. That way you maintain your momentum and your confidence, so you're prepared to use the knowledge you got from the last presentation (which you didn't necessarily close) to be functional in the next presentation.

My sales career was a lot of fun – some said there should have been a movie of me pulling all of this off! It's so incredible to have done it the way I did it, in so many ways. Some naysayers wouldn't believe it, saying, "Oh he couldn't have done that." What the naysayers were really saying was that it wasn't possible for them to pull it off. I didn't care either what they believed. I was there.

The Creative Sales Bible

It's been said that "you can take a Successful Creative Salesperson up in an airplane, hand him a pen, drop him with a parachute, and he will go right to work." His motto is "have pen, will travel." As it turns out, no matter what our station in life may be, we are all at times salespeople when we attempt to promote our ideas and products to others. But to be successful we must first be creative in selling ourselves, thereby making our ideas and products the byproducts of our promotions.

But just what is the definition of a Successful Creative Salesperson? Certainly there are many. As for myself, my ideal is someone who has a commitment, a *personal* commitment. A personal commitment that consists of doing it simple, creating something from nothing with aptitude, attitude, and accountability. Aptitude that comes from the brain and attitude that comes from the heart.

Let's first examine the "attitude" of a Successful Creative Salesperson. It is someone who is motivated within, that is excited with drive and determination. He looks through the eyes of an immigrant who sees the streets paved with gold in the land of milk and money, where there are no guarantees, just opportunity. He deals with risk, reward, recognition, is result oriented, and focused with a passion in the pursuit of profits through excellence. He's impervious to the weeping and whining of naysayers and prophets of doom who talk about strikes, lay-offs, and market drops. He sees the silver lining through adversity, whereby the glass is half full, not half empty. He's a competitive maverick with momentum, whose philosophy is *Do it now! Do it different! Do it daring!* and *Do it simple!* He doesn't wait for something to happen, he makes it happen. The only word he understands is "hustle," as he does his due diligence seeking out leads from cold calls, referrals, and centers of influence.

He has character, charisma, and credibility; he's believable, his word is his bond. He means what he says and he says what he means, realizing that the truth is the refreshing difference. He's perhaps one of the last of the "rugged individualists." He marches to the beat of a different drummer in our cradle to grave society. He's the "right stuff" of what separates a thoroughbred from the Also Ran's who live on yesterday's laurels, until someone asks, "What have you done for me lately?"

Certainly a cut-above the suede shoe, blue sky artists that exist on leads from "back room operations" which are destined to become embellished presentations. He is not a "pro" - he is a *professional*.

The Successful Creative Salesperson with the right attitude and a personal commitment with accountability knows that generally there's three ways to write a deal - luck, talent, or numbers, or a combination of the three.

As we all know the harder we work, the luckier we get. And talent, fortunately or unfortunately, we have or we don't. But numbers - *numbers* - could be the equalizer to talent. It's the Law of Averages: the more people we talk to, the more probability of writing the deal. Numbers could be the salvation for some salespeople. Numbers are infinity. To stretch the point, it's been said that you can take an infinite amount of monkeys, put them on an infinite amount of typewriters, and eventually they would tap out the greatest works ever written. Numbers - if they can work for monkeys, they can work for salespeople.

The Successful Creative Salesperson with the right attitude and a personal commitment with accountability is pragmatic, and at times assumes the worst knowing that the best takes care of itself. He works on bread and butter deals while always in sight of the home run. He or she is not an ego-tripper off with Alice in Wonderland, attempting to write the unwinnable or grief-laden deals. They know when to cut bait and go for the easy one up the street.

The Successful Creative Salesperson with the right attitude and a personal commitment with accountability has what I call a "Teflon stomach," as they are pummeled with rejection, recrimination, and reality.

Rejection, whereby he receives what I call the salesperson's worst nightmare: the cancellation from the prospect who just came out the ether, perhaps influenced by some uninformed deal killer who triggered the buyer's remorse. This is compounded with the "stress" of hearing the word "NO" or "just leave your card; I want to think about it." The salesperson knows that at times the best pitches they will ever make may be the ones they lose, thereby winning the battle but losing the war.

This fosters recrimination and excuses as to what went wrong, until like the priest in the confessional he or she realizes that the best excuse is no excuse. Then, the reality: that in life you have to deal with "what is," not "what should be." They know also that the acid test above all is to get up when you are down. That's why he or is a Successful Creative Salesperson with the right attitude and accountability, doing it simple, leading to a personal commitment in the process of creating something from nothing.

On the other hand, the "aptitude" of a Successful Creative Salesperson begins when he or she visualizes through a "sixth sense" a Master Plan with goals and deadlines that become a self-fulfilling prophecy, and that if it fails they go to Plan B.

Their competent; a street-wise survivor whose been tested in the trenches with a track record. They're able to deal with local as well as global markets. In the process of creating something from nothing, he's on the cutting edge with product knowledge, with a holistic philosophy which is a synergism of body, mind, and spirit.

His modus operandi in a sales setting is to *get control of the situation* first, last, always. He orchestrates what I call the "best performance by an actor, playing many roles."

He's wired for sound and signal, listening to what is said and what is not, which is the difference of omission and commission. He's put on a "clinic," shifting gears and rotating roles from a positive to a negative presentation with rhythm and transition. He's both an iconoclast and a panacea as he infects the belief system of the prospect to illustrate the problem, and conveniently comes up with the cure.

His time, timing, and tone are key. Time: where he becomes the master of the clock, careful not to overstay his welcome. His timing is always in sync, similar to a good comedian's joke. His tone is always sensitive to the situation.

He divides and conquers the prospect with short, punchy, and simple lines, appealing to emotion as well as logic.

They keep in mind William Shakespeare who said that "brevity is the soul of wit."

The Successful Creative Salesperson has the footwork of Ali, disarming and knocking out objections with third person stories that allow licensed. He has the skill of a surgeon utilizing mental surgery to quality and analyze the prospect's value system, careful as he imposes his own so that prospect won't lose face and rebel by closing his wallet. The Successful Creative Salesperson has the cunning of a trail lawyer utilizing "subtle pressure" as he litigates his case. He is unassuming; he starts as a David and ends as a Goliath, proving once again that the pen is mightier than the sword.

Last but not least, the Successful Creative Salesperson with aptitude and accountability, doing it simple, is a *closer*. He presents the hook to the prospect with the closing statement, saying, "What if I could offer you the best quality, the best service, and the best price... is there any reason why I couldn't get your business today?" Then silence is gold, and the first one to talk loses.

And if the prospect accepts the offer, the creative salesperson proceeds to hype their product to a successful conclusion: anti-climatic, with audacity, accountability, with an assumptive close of urgency. And if the prospect's motive for buying was one of greed, and it should exceed skepticism, then they will negotiate a done deal. When the Successful Creative Salesperson requests the prospect to get him a pen, a statement that animates him to the checkbook, he will win what I call the Academy Award.

If on the other hand they should come to an impasse and strike out, he doesn't self-destruct and blow up bridges, but hopefully smile with dignity. He retires to do a skull session on the basics of the presentation to find out just really *who sold who?* He knows that in the end, there's always another day to strut your stuff, and that you never really lose until you admit it. And that's why he or she is a Successful Creative Salesperson with the right attitude and aptitude, with accountability, doing it simple in the process of creating something from nothing that leads to a personal commitment.

Good luck and good selling!

BONUS: The Snake Pit

A bonus! Reader, aren't you so lucky? Here's an excerpt from my book *The Sales Trap*. Enjoy.

Chapter 1
The Snake Pit

"Lead Mooch, like I told you when you first hired in, you can make 30 thou with this deal."

"Yea, but, Blue Skies, how can I score on those bum leads that Old Broad feeds me from the Boiler Room? You're the boss. Straighten her out, or I'll quit. I mean it. I'll quit."

The above heated conversation takes place in a dingy sales correspondence school office. Blue Skies, the sales manager who had been known to con a salesman or two in his time, is trying to placate his number one crybaby, Lead Mooch.

Meanwhile, in the conference room, another discussion is taking place.

"Hey, Hy Binder, catch any live ones lately?" asks Swade Shu, a seasoned veteran of the field as he sits with his feet up on the table. He's sporting a $300 toupee, a suit that costs equally as much, platform shoes for height, full bridge work, and a sun lamp tan that he wears year round to give him the appearance of a younger man.

"Ah, the mooches aren't biting," replies Hy Binder, another pro, stroking his thin mustache while puffing on a stogie. He's flashing a diamond ring on his pinky, belonging to the world's most exclusive fan club, his own. Looking into the mirror on the wall, just below a plaque that shows him as last year's salesman of the month, Hy Binder adjusts his tie, in a somewhat disgusted but vain manner, which quickly changes to cockiness as he says, "I really nailed a hot dog the other night. The guy asked me if after he graduates from the course would the school place him on a job."

"Not another creep that wants us to guarantee life for him?"

"Yep," replies Hy Binder, now filing his fingernails while displaying demonic laughter. "I looked the turkey in the eye and said, 'Of course the school guarantees placement when you're finished. Don't sweat it.' Man, he really bit on that. He gave me a C note as a down stroke and thanked me for five minutes."

"Yes," says Swade Shu, "you really fell into a lay down on that deal."

Hy Binder continues, "Are you kidding me? This clown was so gullible he didn't even bother to ask me who was holding the paper or read the contract."

"That's a riot," says Swade Shu. "The school couldn't guarantee that they would even be in business, what with the heat the new consumer laws put on it, let alone guarantee some student a job. If they did place someone, it would be the first time."

"Well, it looks like you are leading the pack in the contest for the trip to Europe."

"It isn't over yet. Strate Lace is still in the race," says Swade Shu, feigning humility.

"Not only will you take the contest, but also Blue Skies' job when he gets promoted to the home office. Just remember your friends when you get there, pal," says Hy Binder.

"No problem at all," retorts Swade Shu.

Just then the door opens, and in walks Meele Mouth, a fairly new man with a suit that went out of style in the '50's, carrying a briefcase that looks like he was going on a weekend trip instead of to work.

"Hi, fellas," he utters, looking like more of a match for Mickey Mouse and totally out of character with the likes of Hy Binder and Swade Shu, who give each other the eye, putting him on, saying, "I hear you're knocking them dead," in a baiting tone.

"Oh, no," says Meele Mouth to Swade Shu in a sincere and naive way. "I give the people my best sales pitch, but they still don't buy, but they sure think I'm a nice guy." This statement seems to inspire his ego as he stands erect and proud.

Swade Shu fires back, "Sure they think you're a nice guy. That's because when you come down to the close, they know you won't put the bit on them."

"Yes, but I don't want them to get mad at me," quivers Meele Mouth.

Now Hy Binder adds his two cents. "Hey, man, get your act together. Do you think you're out there to win a popularity contest? Nail them, then and there. You're never going to see them again anyway."

"You think I ought to get tougher? Naw, I couldn't do that," says Meele Mouth.

Swade Shu now stands up as if filled with fervor and says, "You have to get tough, you ding-a-ling. Let them know who the boss is. Tell them if they don't buy now, you'll have to disqualify them, and they will lose their opportunity in the future to ever get into the program."

"Hey," replies Meele Mouth, "that's a good idea. I might try that."

Now Hy Binder turns around, points his finger with authority at Meele Mouth, and shouts, "Look, when you're pitching a deal, never mind the kissing the kids and petting the dog. You're there to close a deal. Get that bread right away. If they say they don't have it, tell them, 'Look, I'll tell you what. If you want to show good faith, give me your watch or stereo set to hold until you get the money.'"

"Gee, but they might say I'm high pressuring them."

"So what. They are mooches, and they want to buy," retorts Hy Binder.

"You bet your sweet bippy," says Swade Shu. "If you don't make the decision for them, they will never do it. They ain't got the guts to do it." He continues, "Get tough, but with control."

"Yeah," says Meele Mouth, extremely impressed and fortified, "I will try that. Gee, thanks, fellas."

At this point the door opens again, and in walks Krak R. Baro, a man who has been around more or less a couple of years, wearing a plaid shirt and striped pants, chewing on prunes. "Howdy Doody, guys. How's tricks?"

"Oh, hi there, Krak R. Baro," replies Meele Mouth. "Swade Shu and Hy Binder are teaching me a couple of closes. Gee, they sure know a lot of them."

"Yeah, that's great," replies Krak R. Baro. "I had a deal the other day. The people were fabulous."

"Did you write it?" asks Swade Shu.

"Not yet."

"That's what I thought," laughs Swade Shu.

"But the people told me to come back next week to wrap it up. Things were going so swell that I decided to go to my car and get my banjo from the back seat. I went back into the house, and we all played and sang tunes until two in the morning. Boy, did we have a good time!"

"Can you believe that nut?" asks Hy Binder, looking at Swade Shu.

"Yeah, this guy's something else."

"Oh, that reminds me to get to the bank," says Krak R. Baro. "Hope my wife deposited her check. Gotta keep the wolves from the door. Sure glad she's got a good paying job. You know my philosophy, if you can't make a sale, then go fishing and relax. Oh, by the way, Meele Mouth, I'm thinking about taking some classes in hypnosis, so that I can mesmerize the people to buy."

"Gee, that sounds great! Can I go with you?"

"Sure thing. No problem at all, Meele Mouth. Have a prune."

"Don't mind if I do," and they both leave the room.

Meanwhile, Swade Shu and Hy Binder are still standing there, shaking their heads, as if they couldn't believe what their ears have heard. Hy Binder remarks, "Between the two of them, they couldn't write a deal if it came up and bit them."

"Yeah, real class," smirks Swade Shu.

Both men sit down again and throw their feet back up on the table. Swade Shu whips out the racing form, and Hy Binder pulls over to analyze it with him. No sooner do they do it, then in from the men's john walk another pair of winners. It is Al Truism, the bleeding heart optimist, and Hard Gui, the perpetual pessimist, both fresh recruits, who have just finished their training class and are ready to get in the field to watch a pitch by one of the pros.

"Good morning, gentlemen. How are you? My name is Al Truism," he says, introducing himself in a scholarly manner. "This gentleman beside me also just finished the training."

Now Hard Gui opens up. "What say, man? What's the scam? You guy's making any bread? Who's the top dog here?"

The barrage of questions irritates Hy Binder, who fires back, "My pal Swade Shu is the heavyweight here, and he will take first place in the contest for the trip to Europe. Besides, if you're a pro you can make it anywhere. Right, Swade Shu?"

"Right on, Hy Binder. It's all on how you control the mooches."

"Don't worry, I'll handle them. I could enjoy winning a trip myself," says Hard Gui in an obnoxious manner.

"Gentlemen, really I'm sure you all have the student's best interest at heart," injects Al Truism in a patronizing way, not wanting to accept the callous tone of the conversation.

"Yeah, sure, sure, man," says Hy Binder, winking out of the corner of his eye to Swade Shu.

"The only interest I have in mind is the interest on my coins at the bank," remarks Hard Gui.

"Ho, ho, ho," laughs Al Truism, now injecting levity to again attempt to break up the mercenary statement of Hard Gui.

Hy Binder is so engulfed with the conversation that he ignores the phone ringing on his desk. So, wanting to be an accommodating good fellow, Al Truism picks it up. "ABC Correspondence School of America. Al Truism speaking. Who's calling?" he asks in a very professional manner.

An angry high-pitched voice bellows back, "This is Mrs. McMadd, and I've been trying to get hold of that rascal Hy Binder for a week. He sold me a law course and told me I could be a lawyer in just six months. He lied to me. So I want my money back, or I'm going to cause a big fuss. Is he there?" she asks, in a hostile tone.

"Oh, yes, I'm sure there has been a mistake," says Al Truism, trying to soothe the wounds of the enrollee. "I'll get him."

And before Al Truism can say another word, Hy Binder finally takes notice of the phone conversation and says, as he muffles the phone with his hand, "Who is that?"

"It's Mrs. McMadd, and she wants to speak to you."

"Dummy, don't tell her I'm here. Tell her I'm out of town on business," he whispers to Al Truism, who in turn relays the message.

"Well, when he gets back, tell him to call me right away. Do you understand?" she shouts.

"Yes, ma'am. Yes, ma'am," replies Al Truism, who is somewhat stunned by the conversation.

"Have a nice day," he starts to tell her as the phone is slammed down in his ear. "That dame is an eight ball."

"It's just a slight error," says Hy Binder to Al Truism, trying to cover up the dirt.

"Oh, I'm sure it is," says Al Truism in a perplexed way, trying once again to make light of the events.

"Blue Skies said we could each accompany one of you to observe how the presentation is performed."

"I'm simply overwhelmed with the possibility to help one to improve his mind. Tell you what: Hy Binder and I have some personal business to take care of first. We'll check with you later, to go on a pitch this evening."

"Okay, it's cool with me," replies Hard Gui.

"Very good," says Al Truism. "We will spend the day learning our presentations." And they head to the coffee machine down the hall.

"What planet did this dreamer just land from?" asks Hy Binder out of the side of his mouth.

"I heard from the grapevine that he's a reject from the school system, used to be a teacher. He feels he can get fulfillment here because he thinks education sales is the same thing as a class room," replies Swade Shu, laughing.

"Well, I give this hockey puck about a week before the mooches out there bust his bubble," says Hy Binder.

Both Hy Binder and Swade Shu have traveled the circuit, pedaling home improvements, vacuum cleaners, food plans, encyclopedias, recreational land, grave lots, and used cars. They both know the score, and move on from time to time to the best action they can get. They can spot a pro in a moment. So when a guy like Al Truism hits the scene, they generally have him destined for failure.

"Take Hard Gui with you for your sit, and I'll let Al Truism ride shotgun on mine," says Hy Binder.

"That's all right with me, but you better tip that Al Truism off about opening his mouth during your pitch, or else he might blow your deal."

"Don't worry, I'll muzzle him if necessary. You better cover yourself and straighten out Hard Gui. He looks like the type of turkey that might yap during your pitch."

"Believe me, I'll make it a number one priority," says Swade Shu. "Let's tell these guys that we will be riding in their cars. Why should we spend the dough for gas. They pick our brains to learn the tricks of the trade, just to fade from the deal anyway. We've got to get something for our efforts."

"I also got the poop on Hard Gui. He's a laid off factory worker who's been in the game before. He used to peddle $300 baby carriages with some outfit that skipped town. Friend of mine knows him, says he got zapped right on the nose one night by a prospect for insulting him because the guy didn't buy the deal," says Hy Binder.

"It figures," says Swade Shu, as they both analyze the racing form again.

"Hope I can pick a long shot. I need the break to keep my ex from taking me to court because of back alimony," says Hy Binder. They both start selecting their ponies when in walks Neil Fite, another recruit who has just had his first night in the field.

"Yippee," he yells, "I just wrote my first enrollment! What a fool I was working the last nine years as a clerk, making only $10,000. Hi, guys," he says to Hy Binder and Swade Shu, who don't even bother to look at him. They wonder where he got the deal.

Finally, out of curiosity and envy, Swade Shu asks, "Who did you write, man?"

"Oh, I wrote my brother-in-law on an accounting course," replies Neil Fite.

"That's what I figured," whispers Swade Shu to his buddy on the sly. "It had to be a relative or a lay down." Neil Fite doesn't catch the remark; he is too excited talking about the big money he is going to make in the future.

"I hope this guy's got lots of relatives, otherwise he is going to starve to death in this racket," says Hy Binder. "What a goofy. I hear from Blu Skies that he took a $2,000 sales course. Now he writes his own relative and thinks everything is a bed of roses. I'll make book that he doesn't last any longer than the other clowns, Hard Gui and Al Truism, and runs back to the security of his desk jockey job."

"No doubt about it," agrees Swade Shu, as they both light up cigars, flicking ashes on the floor, and glancing at the racing form.

"Hear the latest scuttle? Strate Lace bagged four deals yesterday."

"Yeah, he probably got lucky and wrote some lay downs," replies Swade Shu, slightly envious.

"Just the same, he could catch you in this last week of the contest."

"No sweat. It's in the bag," says Swade Shu. "What do you say we split down to Bunky's gin mill for a couple of quickies?"

"Might as well. We can't make a buck here," replies Hy Binder, as they leave, tossing the racing form into the basket.

Looking for Chapter 2? Find out who sold who in the book The Sales Trap *by Kenneth F. George*

Notes & Quotes

This is where I poured all of my ideas and thoughts that are included in this book. Some of them may seem repetitious while others will be related to what has already been covered. Consider it a review.

DON'T:

- *Don't* pitch a crowd with a Ringer – they'll blow them all out by saying something negative

- *Don't* pitch a one-legger – if the husband or wife isn't there, they may end up cancelling

- *Don't* play the blame game – if you keep it up, don't bother getting out of bed in the morning

- *Don't* defend – it's suspect. Always agree, disarm, then attack.

- *Don't* stop – or you'll lose your momentum

- *Don't* wait – do it now, do it different, and do it daring

- *Don't* quit – always get up

- *Don't* use sublanguage – the prospect won't know what you're talking about

- *Don't* get sold on the prospect – he's trying to sell you in the idea that he can't be sold

- *Don't* ask someone to buy

- *Don't* say thank you

- *Don't* advance to the second commitment without securing the first

- *Don't* ask for help

- *Never* lose

The only difference between the local crook and some of these salespeople was the thief has a gun and a mask.

A prospect doesn't know you missed something in your pitch until you say something about it and admit it.

I hear quite often in sales that you "have to believe in your product." What a crock! I'm not saying that I believed or didn't believe in it, but if you can pull it off because you believe in you, you could sell snow to an Eskimo.

"The fault lies not in the stars Brutus, but in ourselves." – William Shakespeare

Divide and conquer. Use subtle pressure, gaining each commitment slowly. To close, motivate them to the checkbook by asking for a pen.

You must run the gauntlet of rejection to survive in sales.

Smart is dumb, and dumb is smart

"There's nothing as powerful as an idea whose time has come."
– Victor Hugo

In it, not of it

Buy or lie

You can never lose what you never had

Come out the winner, sale or no sale

If too much knowledge is a dangerous thing, who among us has nothing to fear?

Overcome naysayers

Never wait, time kills

Product doesn't sell, you sell – the product is the byproduct

Successful Creative Salesperson: doer first, thinker second

The harder you work, the luckier you get

Instead of twenty reasons why you can't, give me one good reason why you can

Sales from no sale

Work smart, not hard

Respect first, popularity second

What you see now you may never see again

Never ask for order, take order

Motivated more by #2 spot than by #1

Blame yourself first, not others

Time, timing, and tone

What is said versus what is not

Stop talking, start listening

Who sold who?

The best pitch is the shortest pitch

Salesperson's worst nightmare: cancellation from the prospect

Control begins with yourself first, not the prospect

Control is the key to the close

Work hardest when not pitching

The decision maker is the salesperson, not the prospect

It's harder to take $5,000 from Joe Lunchbucket than $50,000 from a doctor

Silence is gold

It's not a question if you want it, it's a question of if you can get it

Emotion exceeds logic

When greed exceeds skepticism, you have a done deal

Tell me yes, or tell me no

If you're on time, you're late

You never lose until you admit it

Don't let the perfect be the enemy of the good

The best excuse is no excuse

Pay the price to pay the bills

Paralysis by analysis

Use third-person stories – not self – to eliminate objections

Sales is a question of time and numbers

You must have a personal commitment

Never wait: time kills

Don't fill the need, create the need

If I'm wrong you have nothing to lose, but what if I'm right?

Sell, don't get sold

Close your mouth to close the sale

What is not vs. what should be

Don't wait for it to happen, make it happen

Motivated within, not without

Commission vs. omission

Formal power vs. informal power

Assume the worst, the best takes care of itself

It's not the last guy in, it's the last guy standing

Afterword

I'm proud of the fact I consider myself an idea guy even more so than a closer. Creating something from nothing gave me the concepts to close. These ideas have always been out there for anybody, I just took advantage of them.

Reader, by now you've gotten a sense of my general attitude which is a Reverse from the typical salespeopl. Never wait. *Do it now, do it different, and do it daring.* This inspired my personal commitment to be the best that I could be. And if my competitors did not get it, I assure you the prospects did. I would suggest to you budding sales types, if you ask me for advice, I would say try this method. If I'm wrong, what have you lost? But what if I'm right?

The method I utilized in this narrative is a good indication of my modus operandi with the prospects. This is why I never lost. I sincerely hope after reading this book some of you struggling salespeople will find another way of looking at the field of sales.

This is your wake-up call. You lightweight salespeople who didn't write a sale this month, you can now go return the money you paid for this book to the kid's piggy bank or the church collection basket – whichever one you took it from.

And remember this: *The greatest Reverse of all is the truth.*

To the cast of characters that participated in this venture, allow me to thank you for your contribution, whether I wanted it or not – the critics, Sweet Willy, the academic naval gazers, suede shoe closers, prospects, suck-up salespeople, coffee machine crybabies, ex-associate, the guys that burst my balloon about the Easter bunny, the little frustrated nuns, wide-track donut eaters, the rah-rah motivational speakers, and whiners in general. My apologies to anyone who didn't quite make the list. And to all those who did – *gotcha*!

You have the right to criticize my book, right after I read yours. What's that? You didn't write one? Ah, well.

Wow – did I write this stuff?